Creating Your Own Rainbow

R. Palan, PH.D

Published by Advantage, Charleston, South Carolina.
Member of Advantage Media Group.

ISBN: 978-1-59932-064-9
LCCN: 2008921742

Testimonials:

One thing is for certain: If we don't take responsibility for creating our rainbow, we allow other people and circumstances to shape our lives by default. Then we chase that ever elusive rainbow that may never be caught.

Once we move from being a rainbow chaser to a rainbow creator we discover the secret to eternal youth.

You can be just thirty-three and over the hill,
Or ninety-three going on twenty-nine!
Age isn't living a number of years;
It is only a state of mind!
You're never too old to be young,
If you make creating rainbows part of the plan
Because the best thing in life is to die young
As old as you possibly can!

Enjoy the wonderful wisdom and insights of my good friend, Dr. R Palan as he shares how to become a "Rainbow Creator"

Scott Friedman,
President, National Speakers Association,
2004-05, Author of "Punchlines, Pitfalls and Powerful Programs" and "Using Humor for A Change."
www.FunnyScott.com – Scott@FunnyScott.com

'Papa; Look at the rainbow, it's so beautiful!' squealed Soumya, my daughter. Stepping out, I looked around and asked her,'Where is it?' She guided my vision towards the rainbow and I soaked in the visual splendor. As a child, life is alive, with an all pervading sense of wonder and curiosity. Twinkling eyes with trust and hope writ large in them, a child enjoys life thoroughly.

Life too exists with myriad paradoxes and contradictions, and your ability to create your own rainbow in the midst of it comprises the journey of life. As children we are all Rainbow Creators. That ability is lost for a large section of mankind which gets sucked into playing a 'survival game' and loses out on the wonder and enjoyment of being a creator of life.

This book offers practical steps for reconnecting with the creator within and also tickles the soul.

The German poet Goethe asserts

Are you in earnest? Seize this very minute-

Boldness has genius, power and magic in it.

Allow the magic to unfold in your life by boldly moving in the direction of your dreams and 'Create Your Own Rainbow'.

Uday Khedkar,

Life Long Learning, Mumbai, India

The world of thought captured in this book is likely to be popular with the majority of readers. Many may be kind enough to pause a while, breathe deeply a little and offer their company to the author. Dr. Palan has done some bit of outer scanning and inner searching. As a result, he has emerged with essential and practical interpersonal skills that we needed to practice every day leadership – to be a quiet leader.

This is a book that we should bring along everywhere we go. It is a tonic that we need in time of turbulent and challenges as now.

Haji Zulkifly Baharom, FCIPD,
General Council, Malaysian Institute of Management

The rainbow: "the arch of brilliant colours that appears in the sky when the sun shines after a rain shower" metaphorically related to life makes it interesting. Wonderful, colorful, vivid and optimistic picture that I couldn't resist but to follow. His informative guidance, to the end, has navigated the reader towards an interesting journey.

Dr. Abdulrahman Al-Hashemi,
National Drilling Company, United Arab Emirates.

"By sheer coincidence, I met Dr. Palan in 1982 and we became good friends. 23 years later, I had the honour and privilege to be one of the facilitators for "Creating Your Own Rainbow" for an outstanding organization, Singapore Airlines as well as other organizations. Conducting the programme on behalf of Dr. Palan was a great experience. This programme has not only been thoroughly enjoyed by hundreds of participants, it has touched the hearts and lives of many of them. More importantly, I have been inspired and transformed by the success of this programme. I am committed to continue using this programme to help inspire many others for the rest of my life."

Yeo Thiang Swee,
Singapore

Creating Your Own Rainbow

R. Palan, PH.D

Table of Contents

Part Three

Dedicated

To the memory of my grandfather
M.PM. Narayanan Chettiar

A perfect example of a true Rainbow Creator
who epitomized the lines:
"As one lamp lights another, so nobleness
enkindleth nobleness."

Foreword

I was in a busy summer airline flight coming back from KL where I met for the first time, my true mentor and friend. He delivered not only the most enjoyable engrossing and outstanding programme that transformed my career as a trainer but also touched my inner self. In the midst of this busy August flight filled with the sound of infants crying, mothers yapping about their summer shopping fearing their credit bills, men talking about their loans and the investment opportunities they were dreaming of, there I was, totally lost in a world of Dr. Palan's making.

Simple anecdotes and stories that made him the man he is today and how each one of the stories represents the world of experiences for all of us to reflect upon. My whole life ran through my brain like flashlights of sudden awareness. Why this and that happened! and what contributed the making of "me"

I could not heed to the steward's request for dinner nor breakfast because I could not leave this book until I knew whether I was truly a person that 'chases' her dreams or 'makes' them. Upon completion, the smile on my face never parted me for months to come...

When I went back home, there was nobody to whom this book was not recommended to. It has become my best gift to people for years since understanding the true meaning of inner power has been a life-long quest of human-kind in all cultures and generations.

The simple truth to the accomplishments of great people is simplicity itself. Genuine simplicity that transforms a learner from being one who is in quest for knowledge to someone who extends it to humankind at large. And that is the symbol of lifelong learning that I have always found in my dear mentor.

Grab the opportunity that comes to you, not only to learn what I have learnt from my mentor who resides across oceans from my home but who made me visit his hometown every summer of my life thereon. Spread his wisdom to all those you love for sharing knowledge is one of his fundamental values and it is what makes nations rise to greatness and success.

Ms. Amal Ishaq Kooheji
Bahrain Labour Fund
June 2008

Just a Moment…

Before you read any further, let me tell you that this book is written by a person who has not only been exposed to the sharp angularities *of* life but also someone who has learned important lessons *from* them. This book is about the challenges I have faced in my way and the ones that may be standing in *your*s. It is about my experiences I have faced in my life and which you may well be facing now: I have made many decisions; some good, some okay and some lousy ones. You may be also making similar decisions. What I am doing here is sharing with you some positive ideas and insights that have been very useful to me. Some are from my world while others are from the greatest authors of our times.

I do not have all the answers but I hope you may find some of the ideas here helpful in creating your own Rainbow.

There are no short cuts to success. History is full of events where success was determined by hard work and a positive outlook towards life. It is within every one of us to create our own rainbow: All that we need is to believe we can do it.

Good Luck and Best Wishes,

Palan
drpalan@smrhrd.com
July 1998

Note to the Fourth Edition

I have been emotionally overwhelmed by the positive responses to the earlier editions of the book. Many readers expressed thanks for sharing personal experiences but they also wanted to know more about the HOW of creating your own rainbow. I must quickly point out that this is not a HOW to book. It was neither my intention nor the goal of this book. All I had wanted to do when I started to write this book was basically to share my thoughts and experiences with you that you could almost immediately relate to.I have read extensively since the 1999 publication of this book. Though the third edition went out of print eighteen months ago, I have waited this long to put my thoughts together. Combined with my personal experiences and the huge amount of information available out there, I think I am now able to dwell on the subject of HOW in a structured manner. Yet, I have not been able to find the time to write a sequel to Creating Your Own Rainbow.

What I have done while publishing this fourth edition are six things:

- Rework this book by editing the language for readability, added exercises and plugged out the typo errors.

- Make the book more relevant by updating some of the content to reflect current scenarios. Apart from that, I have left the material largely unchanged from the previous editions.

- Make available a Tips book for the busy reader,

- Offer a one day training programme that enables the participant to process the principles of Creating Your Own Rainbow relative to one's own life. Though I have hardly run the training programmes myself in the last two years, I have had two colleagues – Yeo Thiang Swee and Uday Khedkar who have done a great job.

☼ Bring in ideas from three great books. I wrote this book in 1999 at a particularly difficult time. The last eight years have been very learningful and meaningful. Three books have profoundly influenced me since then:-

1. **The Power of NOW** by Eckhart Tolle where I learned the importance of NOW. Thanks to my friend Uday who introduced me to this book.
2. **The Road Less Travelled**, Scott Peck's best seller in one of my long visits to the bookshop where he talked about the difficulties of life and showed us how to deal with them.
3. **Eight Mindful Steps to Happiness** by Bhante Henepola Gunaratana, purchased on one of my visits to the Harvard Coop bookshop.

Many of these ideas add depth to Creating Your Own Rainbow. I have tried to briefly bring in the key principles from these great books into this edition. It is my sincere hope that if and when I write a sequel to Creating Your Own Rainbow, I will incorporate their ideas in greater detail.

☼ I have reorganised this book into three parts.

1. Part One describes the relationship of the Rainbow to life. It focuses on this vision. I have shared the true story of an outstanding individual, who is just like anyone else

but could make a huge difference to the world around him because of his proactive orientation to life.

2. Part Two details each of the seven stages.

3. Part Three highlights the simple action steps towards Creating Your Own Rainbow.

This new and revised edition is a result of my personal commitment to pass on my learning. I hope you will continue to create rainbows for yourself and others.

Thank You

R. Palan
June, 2008

Special Thanks

To friends Elsie Chong and Tony Hoo for persuading me to believe I can make a difference.

To a former colleague Lisa Henningham. who helped me change the way I saw the world.

To my friend, mentor and in-house publisher Dr. Nat for never letting me 'give up' on me.

To my teachers, Jesuit priests Fathers George Maliekal and Leonard Paul for helping me learn that there are no limits to our future if we don't put limits on ourselves.

To my colleague, friend and creative director Khiem for supporting my writing

To my colleagues, especially Agnes, Meiling, Carynn and Gaik for their support.

To my colleagues at SMR Group for their encouragement.

To my mentor Sam Abishegam for his support and mentorship.

To my friend, director and well wisher Tn Hj Ishak for his friendship.

To my friends in Singapore Airlines for giving me the opportunity to share the Rainbow idea.

To the publisher Advantage Media, USA

To my entire family – particularly my mother, wife and children for their forgiving and loving spirit.

part one

Chapter One:

Introduction to Creating Your Own Rainbow

....

"Look deep into nature and then you will understand everything better."

- Albert Einstein

The Lovely Rainbow

Have you seen a rainbow, the arch of brilliant colours that appears in the sky when the sun shines after a rain shower? Haven't you marveled at nature's wonder and been struck by its magnificence? Didn't you experience the deep sense of joy just watching the rainbow even though it appeared just for a very short while? Isn't it an inspiring phenomenon, a beauty waiting to happen under the right conditions? Yet, at times we look at the beautiful coalition of seven colours, without seeing it. We look at something 'out there' but don't see beyond. We are stuck in the routine. Many of us have seen a Rainbow but have not looked beyond.

The Rainbow and Life

Successful people are those who take charge of their lives and build their rainbows. They relate the rainbow to life. The rainbow actively reflects life. It is distinct and specific. It represents beauty, hope, optimism and success. And no one succeeds without dreams, goals and hard work. This is the secret about success. Did you ever know about a successful person who didn't tell you about it?

All of us can create our own rainbows provided we have the two basic needs:

1. The desire to want to create our rainbows and
2. The willingness to learn the skills needed to work towards creating our rainbows.

I have built on the works of many great authors in the field of personal development and brought together diverse experiences. I have used the rainbow as a *metaphor* and related the seven colours of the rainbow to seven steps that relate to *Life Management.* Life Management is an enabling process to make life more meaningful for each person as a totality, it is a vision.

Rainbow Creators

There are two types of people: *Rainbow Creators and Rainbow Chasers*. Rainbow Creators know that the treasure lies within them. They focus their desire and sharpen their skills without putting any constraint on their own imagination. Since the Rainbow as a totality is a vision, Rainbow Creators focus on the seven steps essential for life management to achieve their vision. On the other hand, Rainbow Chasers make their mistakes in assuming that pots of gold are out there somewhere waiting to be found.

The Seven Stages of Life Management

1. **R**ecognising YOU can make a difference

   you hold the key to your success.

2. **A**uthentic Change

   you need to embrace and encourage change for success.

3. **I**nvoke your Determination

   your persistence will drive you towards success.

4. **N**ever give up on yourself: Self Image and Self Suggestions

   your opinion of yourself will decide your success.

5. **B**elieve in Desire and Enthusiasm.

   your passion to achieve your goals is the key to success

6. **O**ptimal Leadership and Adventure

   your ability to lead others with zeal will take you towards your success.

7. **W**illing Love and Encouragement

   your ability to inspire and motivate people are essential ingredients for success.

The Beauty of a Rainbow

The rainbow is simply a brilliant display of colours. When the rain has been heavy, the bow may spread all the way across the sky. Its two ends seem to rest on earth. It leaves behind lasting impressions in your mind and more importantly, a meaning behind it. The rainbow is a colourful vision that is meaningful.

Life and the Rainbow

Life also rests on two ends, on birth and death, on arrival and departure and an interval in between that unfolds in time. A successful life unfolding in time is like the rainbow that offers lasting impressions and a meaning behind it. Successful people lead a life that leaves behind vivid memories.

Legacy

Rainbow Creators leave behind a legacy. Mahatma Gandhi and his non – violence movement in India; Martin Luther King and his civil rights movement in the United States of America and the work of Helen Keller. We remember them even long after they have left this world. We consider these people to be successful because we admire their contributions toward humanity.

Our focus on the seven stages of life management, and the time and effort we put into achieving them will help lead us on the path of success to leave a legacy behind.

Success in Life

What is a successful life? Some say it is:

- a good career,
- acquisition of wealth - money and property,
- a happy family,
- good health, and/or
- an unselfish life.

Success is much more than just anyone of these factors such as acquisition of money. It is a complex reality as it differs from person to person. Remember the famous Frank Sinatra love song: "I don't want to be a millionaire because all I want is you?" To him, success was in finding love.

Robin Sharma asks the question – who will cry when you die? Your answer will pretty much indicate your success.

Clarity

One consistent factor present among all successful people is that they are clear in what they want to achieve in life. They are always passionate about what they do; more often than not they are contributing towards making the world a better place for fellow human beings.

Our success will depend on figuring out what we want in life, how intensely we want it, how hard we want to work for it, and what we want to contribute to the general well being of society.

There are many ways to figure out what we want out of life. We can decide on the basis of our inner convictions, by real life observations, looking at another person's life, personal experiences and an inner drive to be different from others in a positive way. The intensity of our wants and our willingness to work hard to achieve our goals accelerates our drive towards success. Success is deciding what you want, working hard to achieve what you want. Your success is defined by YOU.

"Birds fly over the rainbow,
why then
- oh, why can't I?
If happy little bluebirds fly
beyond the rainbow why,
oh why, can't I"

Lyman Frank Baum

Reflections One

Think of some of the Rainbow Creators and Rainbow Chasers in your life.

Rainbow Creators

____

____

____

____

____

____

____

____

Rainbow Chasers

____

____

____

____

____

____

____

____

List the qualities of a Rainbow Creator and a Rainbow Chaser.

Rainbow Creator

Rainbow Chaser

Chapter Two

Four distinct features of a Rainbow

....

"All that we are is the result of what we have thought."

- The Buddha

We can relate personal success to a Rainbow. There are four distinct features of a Rainbow that relate to life:

1. Blending,
2. Two Bows: The Inner and Outer,
3. Prism, and
4. Completeness.

The Blending

Just as the brilliant colours of the rainbow attract individuals, so is the desire for recognition and success. Everyone wants a life as beautiful as the rainbow. However, it is critical to note that the beauty of the rainbow is due to the blending of the seven colours that appear in each rainbow - violet, indigo, blue, green; yellow, orange and red. The colours blend into each other, into a 'singularity' that illuminates the world.

Do we blend or integrate the seven steps of life management seamlessly? The seamless integration of the seven steps of life management is what differentiates successful and unsuccessful people.

There have been examples of many wealthy people who led very unhappy lives. People with outstanding skills have remained mediocre because they missed the blending of the seven stages of life management.

Very few people are blenders i.e. people who integrate the seven steps of life management into their daily life. Those who are not blenders are known as drifters or stirrers.

Drifters are those who go about life in a mechanical way! There is very little self-reflection. They go about life in a routine way. Just like a boat that drifts in the ocean with no particular direction, the drifters in life wander about with no goals or plans.

Stirrers are those who complain about everything and everyone else except their own weaknesses. They not only drift in life but also have poor self-esteem. They create problems all the time and try to make life miserable for everyone. Stirrers lose their circle of friends gradually.

How many of us have had some quiet time to reflect on what we want? Some questions for us to reflect upon:

- Are you a blender, a drifter or a stirrer?
- Do you blend the seven stages of life management into your daily life or get carried away with one or two things while you forget about the other essentials?
- Do you drift in life without a clear plan?
- Do you stir problems and blame everyone else but yourself for all the problems that affect you?

Connecting with Reality

I have come across people who get into a problem because they are convinced they are the only ones who are correct in this world. They come to the conclusion that the whole world is unjust towards them. These people find it very uncomfortable to accept the fact that they are not correct and for the need to listen to other people. The inability to connect with reality is a major obstacle to their growth.

Self- deception will only make it more painful for us in the future. The inability to connect with reality and to be aware of one's own self often results in the individual living without a purpose.

Rainbow Creators have a clear purpose. They are blenders who want to create their own rainbows besides helping others create their own. They are connected with reality and dare to dream and endeavour to fly in the world of possibilities for they really want to succeed in their own way.

The Two Bows: Inner and Outer

In a rainbow, a complete bow shows two bands of colours. The primary bow is the inner and brighter one. The secondary bow is the outer and less distinct one. Life consists of two bands too - the inner self and the outer self. Psychologists often talk about the primary and secondary needs of people.

Rainbow Creators focus on the need for friendship and love, the need to care for fellow human beings and the need to be connected to what you want in life. When you do that, you create your own rainbow and success automatically follows you. Most of the time we are not governed by our inner self. This is simply because it is not always visible. Just like the outer rainbow, the outer or secondary needs take over sometimes. Materialistic needs dominate our life. Aesop once commented: "Outside show is a poor substitute for inner worth."

When I once asked my father to buy an expensive car to reflect status, he asked me a simple question: "Why do you need it when you can't afford it?" His contention was "Never live your life to please others. Do not try to showcase your life for others. Please yourself not others, it is your life." I understood what he was trying to say - do not pretend to be what you are not and to what you cannot afford.

There is a saying that 'people would rather be complimented for one quality that they do not have rather than for the nine qualities that they do. Creating Your Own Rainbow requires you to be honest with your inner self. You need to be ready to accept feedback from others for self- renewal and recognise that growth is a continuous process.

The Prism

Each colour has a certain wavelength. We see the rainbow when the sun is behind and the rain in front of us. As a ray of sunshine passes through a drop of rain, the water acts like a prism. The ray is bent as it enters the drop and separates into different colours. When it strikes the inner surface of the drop, it is reflected. It is then that you see the true beauty of a rainbow, nature's delight.

Life is very similar. We see our life based on the past though life has to be lived forwards. We often forget that all we have is NOW! We miss the present. As we go through our life experiencing various situations and interactions with people, either the situations or the people or both act like a prism.

They help us grow into better people. People encourage and give us the feedback to grow and develop, to help us create our own rainbow. To achieve our full potential, we need prisms.

Two Jesuit priests who were my schoolteachers, Fathers Leonard Paul and George Maliekal of St. Campion High School, were my prisms. They encouraged me when I was ten years old to go up on the dais to speak in debates and act in dramas. It was a disaster many a time. There was a time when I was playing Hamlet and completely forgot my lines. My teachers would not allow me to be discouraged; they helped me grow with support and feedback.

There were many people who would say that you are lousy. However, my prisms did not let others' label of me become a reality. Les Brown, the dynamic speaker always says – do not let others' perceptions of you become true for you.

It is true that it is not easy to accept feedback. There were moments when I fared poorly in dramas or debates, I would be in tears and angry with myself for not memorising the lines well enough. Sometimes I would be angry with the prompter for not prompting the lines loud enough. There were times when I felt compelled to give up theatre and speech because I felt I had made a complete idiot of myself. In moments like these I could not see beyond the anger or the defensiveness. There were many reasons for me to give up but my school teachers acted as my prisms, they showed me the real and good reasons to stay the course to create my rainbow. They always helped me focus on the present moment and learn from it.

Eckhart Tolle says "Realise deeply that the present moment is all you have. Make NOW the primary focus of your life."

I could relate to that. For my prisms in life, Fathers George Maliekal and Leonard Paul, it was better to learn from the incident then and there. There was never a moment when they would let me give up. There was no such word as 'giving up' in their vocabulary. They taught me to accept tough feedback and helped me learn that giving up without making an effort was cowardice. Today, I realise the value of their support. They developed not only my skills but also, more importantly, my inner self.

Completeness

Though the rainbow is known by different names across the world, its beauty characterises it. In India, the Sanskrit term is "the bow of Indra", Italians call it the 'flashing arch,' the Africans call it the 'bride of the rain,' some others call it 'the girdle of God' and 'the little window in the sky.'

Similarly in life, people define success in so many ways. As we discussed earlier, it is different from person to person.

The common denominator though is a sense of happiness when you achieve what you want. It is about completeness and wholeness. Most of us desire a great family, a progressive career, material wealth and status though we say, we want our life to be successful in all respects.

It is true that very few of us blend the seven steps of life management, focus on our inner self, recognise the power of NOW and use the prisms in our life to create our own Rainbow.

The rainbow helps us see life in a total perspective. It helps us see life from the perspective of seven dimensions. It helps us see life in a different way than we do now.

Narrow perspectives

The human eye is usually able to see only about four or five colours of the rainbow at any one time. In a rainbow; the amount of space each colour takes up on it depends on the size of the raindrop through which the rainbow forms. Similarly, the amount of time we spend on each activity depends on the intensity of our wants. And many of our wants are mostly narrow.

Life is mostly viewed from a narrow perspective: making money or building a career. There are many of us who are so focused on our jobs and the pursuit of material wealth that we do not see the other important things in life. The amount of time we invest or spend on something reflects our lifestyle. We do not seem to be able to prioritise our needs. Not many of us have the time to reflect on what we have done, what we do or what we want. A narrow approach towards life does not result in completeness.

Satisfaction

There are also people who are totally satisfied with what they are. This satisfaction combined with the narrow focus does not enable us to grow. This is what prompted Bernard Shaw to say, "As long as I have a want, there is a reason to live. Satisfaction is deadly." The need to grow does not arise from a satisfied person.

Your goals and actions

An observer on a high mountain is able to see clearly the whole circle of the rainbow when the sun is near the horizon. You can see clearly the value of life if you can see the connection between your actions and your goals. The clouds on the horizon are necessary questions about ourselves that we need to answer before we can create our own rainbows.

YOU

So, in a sense, the key to achieving completeness in your life is just YOU. Yes! You can succeed if YOU want to succeed. Just as the source for a lovely rainbow is the sunlight, which is a combination of the seven colours; the source for creating your rainbow is YOU.

ADAPTING

Life is a journey. Making it complete requires adapting to life and also creating opportunities for change. This is a continuous process. Shakespeare in his play *As You Like It* describes the seven stages of life; right from entering the world as a new born to the stage of old age where we revert to the same infant¬ like stage. At every stage there is a need to adapt to the life stage. Equally important, is the need to create opportunities and become the focus of change as change agents. We also need to lead the change when the situation calls for it. Just as there is a need for us to meet the challenges of the seven stages of life, we need to meet the challenges of the seven stages of life management that are positive determinants to creating our rainbow.

Chapter Three:
The Story of a Rainbow Creator

....

"The world is filled with willing people; some willing to work, the rest willing to let them."

The world is full of stories of people who created their own rainbows. They lived their lives well and left behind a legacy of achievements. They succeeded simply because they blended the seven stages of life management to leave behind a lasting impression of their contribution. Colonel Sanders, in his sixties, succeeding with the Kentucky Fried Chicken recipe is a very popular story. I have no need to go that far.

My Grandfather and His Rainbow

The story of my maternal grandfather, Narayanan Chettiar, and his brother-in-law, Nagappa Chettiar, creating their own rainbows is truly an amazing one. It is a story about people with a desire to succeed and make a difference to the world in which they lived in.

My grandfather was a chronic asthmatic and a very fragile person physically but not emotionally. He managed one of the world's largest leather businesses - India Leather Corporation and with his brother- in-law, the Chrome Leather Corporation. The business employed thousands of people and had offices all over the world. That was in the 1950's. My grandfather could not eat any solid food. He survived only on liquids. Two men had to support him if he wanted to move. He managed his business through the snail mail, telephone and telex. Neither he nor his brother-in-law had any paper qualifications in leather technology but they knew the business. One of them could tell when he saw a piece of skin, the quality of the leather without sending it to the lab for chemical analysis. They did not have money, qualification or other critical resources when they started the business. They were certainly not the most qualified people to run the business.

But, they were not going to let the lack of anything stop them from creating their rainbows.

They blended the seven steps of the life management process, they were honest with their inner selves, and they used their experiences as a prism to learn to have a complete wholesome experience. This helped them create their rainbows; as well as help other people create their own.

Recognising You Can Make a Difference

My grandfather had a single-minded devotion for what he wanted to achieve in life. He tempered this goal with a fierce determination to make a positive contribution to society. What he lacked in resources, he made up for with a clearly defined plan of what he wanted to achieve. The driving purpose in his life was to generate employment. He wanted to make a positive impact on people. He showed the world that, if you wanted, "YOU" have the seeds of greatness in you to make a positive difference. It is up to you to create the opportunities and work towards your rainbow. Just as seeds require nourishment for effective growth, you need to continuously reinforce your thoughts with a 'can do' attitude. Money was not the goal but a means for my grandfather. The real goal was to use the money earned to make a positive contribution to society.

Authentic Change

As a management student, I was amazed at some of the techniques they used to motivate people. Though they had grown up in a totally different environment, they recognised the need to change their style of management to suit the times. Managing a large corporation was different from running a retail shop or a farm. It was a 360-degree change from what they did. They realised the need to change their thinking, their actions and the way they managed people if they were to succeed in creating their own rainbows. They changed their styles to suit the life cycle of the business – growth, maturity, recession time and diversification.

Invoking your Determination

Though I did not have the benefit of working with my grandfather and his brother-in-law, I am proud of the positive ways in which they affected other peoples' lives. To learn more about my grandfather, I talked to the people who worked with him. They told me about his ability to remain focused in what he wanted; This was tempered with a fierce determination to achieve what he wanted. Apparently, he would always say "Never ever give up for nothing is impossible."

Never give up on yourself - Self Image and Self Suggestion

My grandfather and his brother-in-law believed in what they were doing. My grandfather would not allow his poor health or disability to stop him from doing anything that he wanted to do. Other people talked of his disability but he was only interested in discussing his abilities. Together, they created wealth for the society. They believed in themselves and also helped the people who worked for them to believe in their vision. The business made millions and that was all put to good use for the benefit of the community and society.

He believed and often told to the people who worked for them, that the human side of management could lead to high levels of productivity and high levels of commitment. This was the reason why the reporting lines were unbelievably simple. He trusted people for their inherent goodness.

Together with the people they created their rainbows.

Believe in Desire and Enthusiasm

My grandfather's desire and contagious enthusiasm to follow through on what he wanted to achieve in life was superb. There were lots of stories of him looking out for new opportunities and seizing them. What other people thought of as impossible, he saw as an opportunity and proceeded to succeed with unlimited enthusiasm.

Optimal Leadership and Adventure

My grandfather's success was not confined to his business. His ethnic community, his family and his employees accepted him as a true leader who put his people before himself. To him, leadership was about helping people realise their true potential. Success was not just about winning in business; it was much more than that. It was caring for people and helping them to create their Rainbows. It prompted him to venture into uncharted waters in the world of business. My grandfather and his brother-in-law soon expanded internationally when no one else in his circle of friends dared to.

Willing Love and Encouragement

My grandfather believed that loving and caring were essential ingredients for successful relationships. People felt loved, supported and encouraged by my grandfather. He did it in his own way. There were no hugs and kisses but he communicated care and love much better than anyone else. He sacrificed his personal needs to make a difference to other peoples' lives.

Despite his frailty and ill health, which were obstacles, he still visited the workstations everyday demonstrating the importance of Managing by Wandering about (MBWA) in the fifties. Now, of course, Tom Peters has popularised this concept as a management tool, which was basically common sense to my grandfather in the fifties. Professor Richard Boyatzis was the one who remarked that common sense is not necessarily common practice. There were only simple common sense practices, no complex management formula. Talking to people, giving them time and treating them with respect and dignity were common sense to him. He was fond of saying that there are many types of lunacy but there was only one type of sense - common sense.

He valued people for their people skills. For example, there was no restriction on any employee to see my grandfather. He would sit in the garden for two hours in the morning and evening. The employees found it easy to talk to him about their personal lives as well as work. Irrespective of their status - an operator or a manager - they would always be given a cup of coffee or invited for a meal. Food was accessible to everyone. Hospitality was extended as a basic human right. People were given opportunities not charity. The fact that my grandfather, who had never gone to school, could like people for their basic worth and not treat them like things was the reason why his death was mourned by thousands of people.

Creating Your Own Rainbow: Nothing is Permanent

We all make mistakes, so did he? His hope for the business to remain within the family and the lack of management leadership after his demise hastened the company's decline. If only he or his brother-in-law had the benefit of a prism that could have reflected the facts to them more clearly, they could have ensured the selection of professional managers who would have had the leadership capabilities and the passion to make the business a great contributor to humanity. The business could have made a sustained contribution to society. We would have continued to see beautiful rainbows. Perhaps the business would have still been productive.

But the rain had stopped only to be replaced by dryness, and the sunshine had gone only to be replaced by scorching heat. Just as the rainbow is not permanent, my grandfather and his business were not permanent. The rainbow does not exist for eternity. Similarly, nothing in life is permanent.

You need to continue to work on what you have and want. There are many famous companies that are no longer around today. Remember Laker Airways, the London based company that introduced cheap fares and made air travel an affordable necessity. It was a great example to many other successful low cost airlines such as Southwest Airlines in the US, Air Asia in Asia. Laker Airways showed the world low cost air travel is possible. Laker Airways helped millions of people achieve their travel dreams. The company, unfortunately is history today. Nothing can guarantee permanence in this world. Permanence is indeed an illusion but what we can do is to continue to work for the betterment of humanity without letting this bother us. We need to reinvent and stay relevant in a changing world; and work for growth.

Today my grandfather's business remains only as an asset for the family. It is no longer an employer. It makes no specific difference to society or any positive contributions. It is sad that none in the family today share my grandfather's philosophy of making a positive contribution as no one in the family seems to have an idea of what they want other than the sheer pursuit of money. The greedy focus on money has destroyed my grandfather and his brother-in-law's contribution though their legacy stays on through the thousands of Rainbow Creators they helped develop.

The rainbow my grandfather and his brother-in-law created lasted for 30 long years. It, however, disappeared when my grandfather died at the age of 69. His goals also died with him. His life was as beautiful as a rainbow. My only sadness is that it was a short one.

Just like the rainbow is being admired for its beauty, he was admired for his nobility. He was a candle that brought light to thousands of others.

Reflections Two

Think through the purpose of your life

How would you like to be remembered for your life?

part two

The Seven Stages of Life Management

Chapter Four:

Recognising You can make a Difference

....

"It is a funny thing about life, if you refuse to accept anything but the best, you very often get it."

-- Somerset Maugham

YOU

YOU live in a fast paced world

The world that we live in today is probably the fastest and most dynamic society in the history of mankind. The pace of change is amazing and it seems that most of the time we are neither able to direct nor control it. Sometimes, life resembles a battleground. And, in this battleground, the most decisive battles are fought within YOU.

The important person in this fast world is YOU.

The person you need to face up to be successful in this world is YOU. You are responsible for creating your own rainbow. A successful life starts with you. You have to recognise beyond any doubt that you are the one who can make a difference to yourself and to the world in which you live.

Personal Accountability

Personal Accountability starts with recognising you can make a difference. Many of us talk about a positive attitude but a positive attitude emerges from personal accountability.

There is a saying that there is little difference among people. However, that little difference can make a big difference. The little difference is attitude and the big difference is whether it is positive or negative. You can either see roses with thorns or thorns with roses. You can see the world either as one of possibilities or one of problems.

And, you are the one who will decide how you see things. A positive attitude will only accelerate your success.

Well, creating your own rainbow is all about YOU. A successful life starts with you. It involves not only your well being but also the extent to which you impact other people's lives and influence situations that lead to the betterment of society. YOU can make a difference to yourself and to the world in which you live.

What does it mean? Making a difference does not simply mean being different for the sake of being different. It does not mean wearing designer clothes to stand out in a party. Neither does it mean driving a Mercedes when your colleagues drive a cheaper car.

It means standing out in a world that promotes sameness and uniformity. It is about creating a positive identity for yourself. You do not have to be famous to do that. It is about your inner self that drives you to achieve what you want in life even when everything else seems to be going against what you believe.

Psychiatrist Dr. Victor Frankl proved that while languishing in the concentration camps of Adolf Hitler. He proved that as long as your attitude is strong, no one can control your thoughts and actions.

Believe in Possibilities

It is about blending the seven stages of life management to impact people and society through your innovation, caring, influencing and sacrificing approaches. It is about following your inner self to make a positive contribution to the world that we live in. It is about being a prism for other people to shine through, to see their seven components and grow positively. It is about living a complete life and helping others to do so. The ability to make an impact on other people by caring for and supporting them to achieve their rainbow separates you from the pack.

YOU alone hold the key to making a difference to your life as well as to other people's lives. This requires possibility thinking. Ask yourself a few questions:

- How do I remain positive in a world that is dominated by negativity?
- In a rapidly changing world, how do I influence the direction of my life?
- At times, when my whole world looks down, what do I do to look up?
- How do I make a difference to the lives of my colleagues, friends and loved ones?
- How can I contribute to the betterment of society?

The key to remaining positive, maintaining a strong belief in yourself and staying motivated when everything else seems to be down is YOU.

YOU HAVE THE POWER OF CHOICE

YOU are accountable for your life; you can choose your actions and you have to help yourself. You have the power to make a difference. Do not give away the power just because someone else says that your choice is not right. And, do not believe that you, as an individual, cannot contribute to the society.

Do you know the story of the smiley face or the name Harvey Ball? Have you heard of him? He's a graphic designer who lives in Massachusetts, United States of America. He's neither rich nor famous but he should be.

Ball created the 'smiley face' - the round yellow head with two raisin-shaped eyes and a big grin. The State Mutual Life Assurance Company commissioned him to draw an upbeat icon to boost the employee morale. The company paid him US$45. They did not register a trademark of the symbol. Neither did he. Subsequent entrepreneurs made millions out of the upbeat icon. Is Ball bitter? No. He says: "I made the whole world smile. Have a nice day." Wasn't Ball happy that he made a substantial contribution to the world through his innovation despite not making huge sums of money? Didn't he remain positive even though he had not made substantial financial gains with his design? There was no remorse or sulking just because he had not made more money. He decided to remain upbeat and happy about his contribution.

Thinking Differently

I only realised that my success can be attributed to my actions and how I see things after I attended a convention on Human Issues. The year was 1979. I was in college and I was delighted to have the opportunity to attend a major conference organised by the youth foundation REACH. The attendees numbered over 200. The participants were eagerly awaiting a panel discussion that featured film directors, psychologists, managers and religious leaders. The discussion revolved around human problems.

The intense debate focused on the negative influences generated by films - the violence, the pornography, the lack of concern for social issues and the diminishing role of personal accountability. At that point, one of the film directors remarked: "I am the product of a five minute idiotic activity of my parents and therefore my actions are governed by the environment. If the masses want violence, the films will have violence." There was a hushed silence among the audience.

However, Jesuit priest Father Fernandez interrupted: "I disagree, Mr. Film Director. I am the symbol of a fusion of love. I am one in a hundred million miracles. I can make a positive contribution to society. Mr. Film Director, let us not talk about what others are doing for commercial reasons. Let us talk about what you and I can do to make a positive difference to this world. Let us influence people in a positive way."

It is nearly 30 years since I heard those words but they still ring clearly in my mind. The words influenced me to think differently and positively. YOU hold the key to how you see the world. You have the Power of Choice. You are personally accountable for your actions and you can make a difference.

Most books talk about the great superstars who went out to get what they wanted but let us not forget that creating our own rainbow is within the reach of each one of us and is purely a personal process.

Caring for other people

People talk about superstars. I remember the so-called ordinary people who have made an extraordinary contribution to society. They have impacted other people by their caring in more ways that we can imagine.

People always ask what difference one individual's effort to care for others can make. I remember what my primary school teacher, Mrs. Smith said "Son, little drops of water make up the ocean." This also reminds me of the popular story on the speaking circuit of the old woman on the beach throwing starfish back into the sea. On being confronted by a young man on what she was trying to do, she responded: "Just trying to make a difference." The young man remarked: "You must be out of your mind. Throwing a few starfish back into the ocean is not going to be a big deal." The old woman responded: "You think so, well, just hold on." She picked up another starfish, threw it back into the ocean and then said: "Well, young man, it sure made a big difference to that one."

My teacher, Professor T.K. Nair, is another example that you do not have to be famous to care for other people. On his retirement, he chose not to work in a high paying job but with the aged people in the metropolitan city of Madras, India. He wanted to care for the old and make a contribution. The goal was to help the aged continue with their lives.

As a young student, I could never understand such actions. After all, life was already difficult enough just looking after yourself and your family. Why complicate it further? There was many a time then when I wondered if such actions were social advocacy and idealist, unrealistic attempts. There were people who agreed with me. Some complained about such idiosyncrasies of people. Professor T.K. Nair might have had all of the human failings but no one could deny his commitment to the causes he truly believed in. He is certainly a person who is passionate about what he wants to do. I met him first in 1977. Today, after nearly three decades, he has not given up pursuing his goals.

I wonder if 2006 Nobel Prize winner Muhammad Yunus and his Grameen Bank experiment in Bangladesh would have succeeded if he had doubted his ability or the micro credit revolution. Such extraordinary contributions from ordinary people make a big difference. Their Nobel Prize for most Rainbow Creators come not from the Nobel Prize committee but from the satisfaction that they have made a difference to society. There was no fanfare about their work when they started out.

The goal of their work is not publicity but the contribution they make to society.

I was touched by the humility of some of my teachers. Professor T.K. Nair wrote to me after reading one of my books: "Children outgrow parents and students surpass their teachers. You are one of those who make the teacher in me proud."

His humility and thoughtfulness in writing me a personal card was touching especially since I was not particularly close to him at the University. There was no way I had surpassed his skills or knowledge but then I realised that that was the greatness of a teacher - to continue to be a prism and motivate students. The meaning of caring, sharing, motivation, humility and greatness cannot be talked about; it has to be lived. Great people do not call themselves great but they have greatness and power bestowed upon them, often after a life time of contribution.

Let me tell you about another friend, Tuan Haji A. Muhammad Isa. He is a motivational speaker par excellence who really believes he can make a positive difference in the lives of other people. He was often called the Malaysian Ambassador of Motivation. He is one who truly believes that people have the seeds of greatness within themselves. I had the privilege of hearing Haji Isa speaking to a group of executives on Positive Thinking. The executives put up all the obstacles and negative questions. All that Haji Isa had to say was "Just hold on, the difference between all of you and successful entrepreneurs is that while you see all the reasons it can't be done, successful entrepreneurs see all the reasons why it can be done".

Did you see the film Mr. Holland's Opus? You should if you haven't. Its poignancy moved me. Mr. Holland fails in his bid to gain popularity as a musician. Though disappointed, he uses his skills to help students learn music. He makes them love music. Though an ordinary schoolteacher, he helps to build students with well rounded personalities. The way he impacts the students gains him eternal stardom in their hearts. His Emmy award came from his students. He created his rainbow by making a difference to the students and by helping them create their own rainbow.

The fact that almost anyone can influence other people can be best illustrated by the work of the students at the Madras School of Social Work in the late seventies. Their fieldwork involved community service work in the slums of Madras, India. Slums are large communities of people living on pavements or large tracts of land with hardly any public amenities. All that the people have is a hut. The lack of employment in the city or poor wages force the poor people to live in slums as they cannot afford better living conditions. Even though the government had a Slum Clearance Board, it was helpless. There were hardly any funds to provide even the basic amenities.

The students were struck by an idea. They realised they may not be able to change the living conditions totally but could make a small difference to end the indignity and the hunger of the poor people living in slums that they chose to adopt. The students went around schools in Chennai, met the principals and asked each student to donate an old newspaper. The collection of old newspapers was sold to the paper mills that recycle paper. The students were able to collect some money, which was used to provide some basic amenities to overcome the abject poverty in the slums. Each student only contributed an old newspaper but that went a long way to satisfying the hunger of many poor people in the slums. The students demonstrated the fact that you do not have to be in government or be rich to help people.

I remember a conversation with a communist sympathiser. To her, such actions only reinforced the system of helplessness and such half hearted attempts treating the symptoms, without addressing the structural problems are grossly inadequate and unhelpful. True enough, we need to address the root cause but can't each one of us start doing something for a start.

All of us can contribute to the world in which we live in our own ways. I have read about a person who dedicates Sundays to planting trees. If she misses a Sunday, she makes sure she makes up for the Sunday missed. She 'sacrifices' her valuable time to make a positive contribution to society. You may wonder if she is going to green the earth, just by herself. That certainly is not what she thinks. She may not be able to stop the powers that are determined to destroy the environment but she can certainly contribute in her own way towards the protection of the environment. If only every person had the same aspirations towards the environment, the world would be a much better place to live in.

This was what Martin Luther King set out to do as a young man. He wanted America to be a better place to live in. He cared for his people. The remarkable life story of Martin Luther King, the civil rights leader and Nobel Peace Prize recipient, moves you when you read about the contributions he made for his people. He sacrificed his life to give hope to millions not only in America but also around the world. At the age of 28, King emulated Mahatma Gandhi's non-violence movement and organised the first large-scale non-violent resistance in America. The Montgomery bus boycott protest that began as a bus strike ended as a Supreme Court decision. It ended the indignity of segregation. His famous speech: "I have a dream" not, only motivated the people then but also reinforces, even today, the right of every person not to be segregated on the basis of colour, race, sex, religion or creed, and to have a dream.

The vision of one man

President Nelson Mandela spent 27 years in prison. He is just like any one of us but what separates most of us from him is his vision that he can make a difference to his people.

President Nelson Mandela spent a lifetime in prison. That did not deter him from fighting for a cause that he believed was a basic human right. To many people he was a symbol of hope for the millions of black South Africans. He was fighting to make a difference in their lives. To my colleague Jeremy and me, he was a symbol of faith for the entire world. He showed that even though people can beat you up, imprison you for a lifetime and torture you, they still cannot buy your beliefs and values.

His errors of judgment are amply offset by his personal integrity, his sense of humour, his forgiveness of human frailty, his generosity of spirit, his faith in reconciliation and above all, the personal sacrifices he has made. He helped his people in the 'the rediscovery of the ordinary,' as writer Njabulo Ndebelee says. His people found freedom, a basic human right. He got his people to recognise two issues: the need to face the truth about the past and the need to reconcile the almost irreconcilable. One man created the Rainbow - a free South Africa where everyone, irrespective of colour, could live freely.

People like Mandela, Martin Luther King and Dr. Victor Frankl showed us that when you believe in something, just never, ever give up. People like Mandela could have easily walked away with a fortune and lived comfortably for the rest of his life. Did he do that? No, he chose to sacrifice his life and suffer for a lifetime so that other people would benefit from his sufferings. He chose to fight the cruel apartheid regime until he ended it. He chose to make the lives of others different i.e. more just.

Jeremy and I had the opportunity to have lunch with President Nelson Mandela. Of course, there were three hundred others at the banquet. We just wanted to see him and experience the feeling of greatness. To our surprise, he was an old man who looked weak and frail yet he was the strong man in fighting the cruel apartheid system. People are not born great; they are bestowed greatness when they make a contribution to humanity. It is about the work you do for your lifetime. There are no shortcuts to creating your own rainbow. There is a famous saying: "As you sow, so shall you reap." We have to first invest before thinking about the returns.

The youngest American President, John F Kennedy urged people to ask not what the country can do for them but instead ask what they can do for the country. His philosophy was simple. Contribute first and the rewards will follow. Remember what he said on his inaugural address "we place our trust in God but knowing fully well God's work on earth must truly be our own."

Often, the work that you do does not bring about instant results. You do what you believe is right. You try to make a positive difference. After a lifetime of hard work you find that you have made a valuable contribution. And a great difference. Things that you do 'now' often comes back to you in the 'future'.

This is best described by a popular story.

The life of the great pianist Ignacy Paderewski. He realised the impact of helping people, 30 years after the incident. Two young men working through Stanford University had difficulty paying their tuition fees and boarding expenses. To overcome their problem, they came up with the idea of engaging the great pianist for a recital. The pianist's manager required a guarantee fee of US$2000. As much as they tried, they could only generate US$I600. After the concert, the two young men had to tell the great pianist the bad news. They gave him the entire collection of US$I600 and a promissory note for the remaining US$400. Though it looked like a financial disaster and the end of their college careers, they promised the great pianist that they would remit the balance at the earliest opportunity. "No, young men that will not do. I am tearing up this promissory note now. I want you to take out of this US$1600, all your expenses and keep for each of you ten percent. Then, let me have 'the rest." Many years passed and when World War 1 ended, Paderewski, now the Premier of Poland, had great difficulty feeding his people, his starving population. Only Herbert Hoover, who was heading the US Food and Relief Bureau, could help by sending emergency food. After the famine, Paderewski travelled all the way to personally thank Herbert Hoover for the emergency relief food. Herbert Hoover replied: "That is all right Mr. Paderewski. You may not remember it; you sacrificed part of your earnings and helped me out of trouble when I was a student at Stanford University."

None of these people were famous when they started out on their mission. They were not international celebrities then. They became great after a lifetime of contribution to society.

All of us have the capability to make a difference. We can improve the service we provide and we can substantially improve the quality of what we do, if we choose to do it. There are numerous stories about what people have done. I can just draw upon the stories of friends and colleagues who joined us many years ago when we were small and grew with us.

There were customers who were worried hiring us because we were not big enough. We continued to work hard to expand our business and seek all the recognition we could.

They may not have had the qualifications to do the job but they did have the dedication. They did not have the best memory but in my memory, they were most passionate and hardworking people. They made a difference in doing their best to help others learn and perform.

What do YOU Think?

Professor T.K. Nair, Tuan Haji Muhammad Isa, Mr. Holland, the students of the Madras School of Social Work or my colleagues were not rich people but they certainly made a rich contribution. They are not Presidents or Prime Ministers but their contribution as ordinary citizens - teachers, entrepreneurs and colleagues - were no less significant.

Harvey Ball, Mahatma Gandhi, Martin Luther King, Nelson Mandela, Viktor Frankl and Ignacy Paderewski were not born great. By being different and making a difference to the life of others, they made an impact on other people by innovating, by influencing thinking and by caring and sacrificing. People were able to create their own rainbows because of their support. As the Indian author and motivational speaker Shiv Khera says "Winners don't think differently, they do things differently".

Can you make a difference to your life, to others and to humanity? Do you believe you have it in YOU to create your own rainbow? It is what you believe? After all, didn't the great Henry Ford say: "If you think you can or if you think you cannot, either way, you are right" YOU can make a difference not only to yourself but also to the betterment of your loved ones and the world in which you live.

Creating Your Own Rainbow is all about you.

You are the STAR...

To say you're unimportant,
Is simply not true,
You are here
That is proof, you are a miracle

Life may be painful and hazy
But there will be a day when you will see
Happiness and Peace
Is truly a possibility

Nature published a book that is you
That's all you need to know
Don't dwell on the past
For you have the present

You have the choice
To experience the Power of Now
Become a Rainbow Creator
Remember, every person is a best seller.

Be proud of who you are
Your character is important
You can make a difference to this world
In your book you are the STAR.

Chapter Five:
Authentic Change

....

"You need to be the change that you wish to see in this world."

--Mahatma Gandhi

Change dynamics

We learn almost on a daily basis that change is the only constant in this world today. Rainbow creators recognise that we live in a world that is changing by the minute. They do not watch the world go by and wonder what happened. They make a proactive contribution. Standing still in a continually changing world does not take you anywhere. It only makes your position precarious. For personal change to take place for personal growth, you need to be honest and take action. This is why Rainbow Creators insist on authentic change. The ability to deal with change starts with us.

Acknowledge what needs to be changed

Change is one of the most talked about subjects today. Yet, very few of us recognise that the first thing we can do is to acknowledge within each one of us for the need to change. Change starts with each one of us.

If we asked a question what needs to be changed in an organisation to improve productivity, very few respond – ME. Often, it is about other things.

Without acknowledging for the need to change and not recognising that change starts with us first, there will be no progress.

Change in Today's World

Not everything that is faced can be changed or needs to be changed, but nothing can be done about what needs to be changed until it is faced. When we talk about change, two questions spring to our mind.

- What can be changed?
- What cannot be changed?

In today's world, characterised by rapid change, where the entire world seems to be turning into a global village, we have to respond to some of the changes quickly and in a positive way. A positive change can make the world a much better place to live in. There is much more to be gained by embracing positive change rather than resisting or rationalising the refusal to change with the times.

Any change that leads to improvement needs to be responded to proactively. To say "This is the way I have been for the last 30 years and this is the way I will continue to be" is a handy motto for delusion rather than improvement in today's world.

If we resist or refuse to change when it is positive, it does not really matter. What matters will be the fact that the entire world around us would have changed and that would result in us also undergoing change not for the better but for the worse. Take the example of learning new ways of working. If you think learning stopped at school and there is no need to learn anymore, you are going to be left behind in this competitive world.

However, before we are branded as pure opportunists, we also need to consider issues that cannot be changed. Universal values such as goodness, kindness and tolerance cannot be thrown overboard just because the world is moving fast and becoming highly instrumental and materialistic. Certain elements of character that promote the human spirit should not be changed.

Change is dynamic and has always been with us, though the pace of change today is comparatively rapid. Just visit the school that you went to and you may find the school and the entire town changed completely beyond recognition. Development might have altered your familiar landscape but that does not change the affection that you may have for your school. Some things change, some just cannot and don't even in a fast paced changing world.

Talking about the pace of change, it is important to remember while it took many years to enroll one million telephone subscribers it took a lot less years to get one million personal computer users. The Internet was much quicker, the mobile phones even faster and the IPod surpassed all of that. Trade barriers are breaking down; people are calling themselves "netizens" with the advent of the post-information technology revolution - the Internet revolution. This kind of pace requires us to keep with the changes if we do not wish to become obsolete. If we wish to remain relevant in today's world, it will require lifelong learning, adjusting our lifestyles and staying productive in a world that does not stay still.

Change presents
new opportunities
for growth

When we ponder over the simple question of what change is, we can think of several answers. Change is a new way of doing things. It is improving the ways we have been doing things. It should lead to the betterment of the individual and society. The goal is to improve the world that we live in.

It is neither indiscriminate change nor about compromising our value systems. Though change is dynamic, we still hold dearly to some values that we cherish. The values of freedom, honesty and trust cannot be thrown overboard just because the world is changing rapidly. Change must have a purpose and it must take us towards creating our own rainbows?" Rainbow Creators love change but do not like being changed – there is a big difference here. Change for betterment is something that we all need to do but being changed without adherence to universal values really means we are compromising our inherent values.

The King of Thailand, in his 1997 New Year address to the people of Thailand, stressed that information technology alone will not promote goodness. It is a tool for people and it is people who promote positive values and goodness ultimately

The need to improve our work productivity requires us to change the way we work which requires us to learn new tools such as the personal computer. However, it does not mean just because we use computers at the workplace, we stop communicating with people. There are numerous instances where colleagues sitting next to one another send e-mails when all that is needed is to just talk to the other person across the desks. This is certainly dehumanising the workplace. On the contrary, there are also people who complain about the Internet or blogs. We cannot deny the positive changes

Information Technology has brought to this world. It has completely revolutionised the world we live in. You can have any information you need within a couple of seconds, right at your desktop with a Google search. However, the Internet has also brought about fear. It also gives you access to unpalatable information.

This is one of the prime reasons for the need to differentiate between positive change and changes that are harmful to the core of humanity. Progressive organisations and nations today emphasise the need for values and ethics in a changing world.

We need a change plan too. The rapid pace of change today has the potential to create chaos and confusion. This may be unbearable and inconvenient but they can contribute to innovation if the change plan is planned and communicated to everyone involved.

Some years ago we were a small operation dedicated to serving at any time, about three customers. When we expanded, it was really chaotic. Though we had more staff, serving 50 customers was far more demanding. Though we put in the required systems, it was still not easy. It prompted my colleague Jeremy Spoor to say: "We need to learn on how to thrive on chaos." We will never have a clearly drafted plan that will survive all changes. This does not mean we forget planning totally. The goal is to balance planning with uncertainties caused by change and to deal with them to a certain extent. It will be impossible to structure everything unless we live in a dictatorial world, which of course will stifle the human spirit. Professor Moshe Rubenstein calls for adaptive planning.

One of the major causes for resistance to change is the fear of the unknown. As much as we may try to predict the unknown, it will still create problems, as there will be issues that cannot be planned because we do not have enough information about them. This brings up two issues in change: ***managing risks and spontaneous responses*** in the change process.

My father was a great planner. He had planned most things to the last detail but he did not calculate risks effectively due to many unpredictable factors in his business. All his carefully crafted plans were in disarray when the economy went into a recession in the sixties. Unable to cope with the stress brought about by the mounting losses, my father succumbed to a heart attack. We could not believe he had died. His abrupt death shocked us to the core. The fact that 'he was gone' was only evident when the bills had to be paid at the end of the month. Ironically we learned from that experience that death is what provides meaning to life. The death of my father induced dramatic changes in our lives. The grief was painful but we still learned many positive lessons. For a start, we learned to support one another much more than when he was alive. The bonds of friendship and love within the family strengthened considerably. Change gives meaning to life.

His death also reminded us that ***life is temporary***. We are not immortal. His death changed my family and me. We had to take total responsibility. There was no one to pass the buck to. The sole breadwinner was gone. The pocket money was gone; there was no dad to turn to and the future looked bleak. There were no holidays or picnics. The weekends were spent trying to figure out how to survive the next week. The changed scenario frightened us, as we just did not know what the future would be for me and my siblings.

It is in times of adversity, that opportunities present themselves. In this difficult time, my mother provided leadership, support and encouragement. Her role changed from one of passive dependence to one of active and independent leadership. Though it often looked like we would not survive one week, we learned from experience that change presented new opportunities for growth. My mother was always focused; she did not waiver for a moment in providing every child with a professional education. Her actions were always focused in that direction. That determined focus on learning stemmed from the unfortunate death of my father.

The experience of the change that we went through helped us develop into more resilient people. We understood change for we had lived through the depth of change. It gave us an insight into the reality and impact of change. We were in the eye of the storm. It was no more an intellectual discussion; we had just come out of a harrowing experience, one where we had learned valuable lessons.

Status quo is comfortable and makes us feel safe from unbearable uncertainties. Changes require us to adjust to new situations, people and processes. It introduces new risks that may be very inconvenient. We prefer to do things that we have always done. It is much more difficult to do new things that we are not used to or uncomfortable with. Change creates discomfort. Rainbow Creators adapt to this discomfort, look for opportunities in change and embrace change for their betterment. They are future oriented and plan for the long run. Rainbow Creators see uncertainties as stepping-stones to success.

Most of us worry; feel sad and anxious about what the changed situation holds for us. There are times when it looks like we are about to succeed only to find that the whole scenario has changed completely. We need to change our strategy, tools and approaches and start all over again. Some people call this a failure. Rainbow Creators call this as a ***learning opportunity***. They make the needed changes and start all over again. They will never give up creating their own rainbows. After all, didn't the Wright brothers learn from mistakes and make continuous changes until they were able to create the flying machine? An inability to adapt to the discomfort caused by change leads to a lot of worries and anxiety.

I had the privilege of meeting Dr Koon, a Singapore child psychiatrist, at one my workshops. He introduced me to the acronym SADS. Failure to change leads to helplessness and sadness when the environment changes. The inability to cope with this helplessness leads to anxiety, depression and finally suicide if we are unable to cope with the change. Change can be painful particularly when we have to give up doing things that we have done for years. So, most of us employ a defence mechanism to cope with our anxieties. We play a game of deception with ourselves.

It may sound very familiar. We always say: It will be different when

- I get a decent job,
- I am married.
- I make more money
- I pass my examinations.
- I have children.
- I stop smoking.

Such actions do not take you towards your Rainbow. If we do not take positive action, time will pass by and nothing will happen. We need to know where we want to go, take charge of our life and believe that luck is the crossroad where preparation and opportunity meet. Rainbow Creators do not postpone change; they flow with change seamlessly.

Managing Change

Managing change requires us to be aligned with the changes in the world and connect our actions with our purpose in life. We need to be positive and ready to learn. Alvin Toffler, the futurist said: "The illiterate of the year 2000 will not be the person who cannot read or write but the person who is unable to unlearn, learn and relearn on a continuous basis."

A positive mindset and a willingness to learn relevant new skills in today's world must precede all other change factors. Change Management requires two factors:

1. Focus and
2. Action

We rarely anticipate and prepare ourselves for change. Are you a Rainbow Chaser or a Rainbow Creator? Rainbow Chasers always attribute the reasons for failure to the changes that happened abruptly. They look at issues outside of their control. Rainbow Creators are people who embrace the change and respond to the change in a productive way. They bring about change. They look within themselves and see change as betterment for themselves and society. They have a clear change plan, which originates from a clear focus.

Focus

A clear focus will enable us to be single minded in our goals. This will help us achieve what we want. It will minimise our wandering through life with a lot of expectations but without any direction.

When factors such as the environment or the tools at work change because of global trends, a clear focus helps us identify the changes that we personally have to undergo in order to create our Rainbow. The focus helps us to take the needed actions. On the contrary, a lack of focus will be a serious obstacle as we are not able to anticipate or respond to change. It will result in us not being proactive but instead reacting in a negative way such as withdrawing into our shells.

There is an interesting episode from the Indian mythological epic Mahabharata. The teacher asks three soldiers to take aim at a bird and asks each one of them a question before ordering them to shoot. The question was "what do you see?" Each one of them had different responses. One said he saw a bird on a tree amidst the forest; the second said she saw a bird on the branch of a tree while the third one said he saw the sharp eyes of the bird. Who among the three do you think was focused?

Many books on self improvement have inspired me. They emphasise the importance of clear goals. The central message in most if not all books is to know what you want. They ask questions such as:

- What is the purpose of your life?
- What do you want to contribute towards humanity?
- What are the changes that you will bring or that will affect you?

Unless you have clear goals, you will have no idea of the impact of these changes on you or the impact of the ones you created. When a person is ready to meet the challenges of change, he or she will be better placed to achieve his/her goals.

Equally important is the issue of implementing our thoughts. In human beings, there is a gap between thoughts and action. For proper relationships between thought and action, one needs to manage this gap productively. This will enable the action taken after focused thought to be very effective. We may have good intentions but we seldom act on them quick enough. A person with a clear focus is able to implement changes quickly. A clear focus hinges on three factors:

1. Self Reflection
2. Clear Thinking, and
3. Clear Goals

Self Reflection

We spend time doing much routine work but we do not seem to find the time for planning to meet the challenges of change. Taking time out to prepare for changes may first seem unproductive but it can be the most valuable few moments of your life. Take time out to ask yourself a few questions:

- What is it that I want in life?
- What are some of the changes affecting the world, society at large and, as a result, me?
- What are the personal changes that I need to make to create my rainbow?

Self-reflection helps us to think of what we want in life. It helps us to prioritise our goals and enable us to focus clearly.

An office colleague with a very traditional approach who was so used to doing things manually found it extremely difficult to change. With automation affecting every part of the business and flatter structures within the company, our colleague realised the importance of learning as the nature of our business required us to look at reports almost instantaneously. The awareness for the need to learn was good but it had to be followed up with action. A positive environment where other colleagues are willing to help contributes to promoting the desire to change. But the response to change and learning had to first come from the person.

Clear Thinking

Zig Ziglar, the motivational speaker commented "If you wish to change the action, you need to change the thinking." The whole world was convinced that the only way to fight the forces of colonialism and racism was through violent means. Mahatma Gandhi and Martin Luther King changed that thinking. They proved to the world that the power of non-violence was far greater than violence, particularly in bringing about change. They were very clear in their minds about the power of non-violence. Non-violence brought freedom to 800 million Indians and later to 24 million African Americans.

Your actions originate from a clear focus. A clear focus is a result of self-reflection, clear thinking and clear goals. When our thinking is erroneous, our focus becomes unclear too. The way we see things may not be appropriate. Rainbow Creators continually ask of themselves if their thinking is compatible with their goals.

There are people who set lofty goals but think of work as a chore. We look forward to Friday, to saying: "Thank God, it's Friday." Our thinking of our work determines our response. I do not think Nobel Laureate Muhammad Yunus thinks of his work as a chore. He sees it as a contribution.

Recently I had the opportunity of meeting a trainer who works with parents. She helps parents develop better relationship with their children. At one workshop a parent remarked: "We brought them to this world, we just cannot control them. Why can't they listen to us?" I was pleased when the trainer quoted the famous words' of Khalil Gibran: "You did not bring the children to this world; they came through you to this world. Do not control them but seek to understand them first." It all depends on how you see your children and what you think of them. I approached the trainer after the session as I wanted to know what she hoped to achieve with the parents attending the workshop. She said: "I just want them to change their thinking from one of control to one of love." Remember Stephen Covey's words – Seek to understand before being understood.

On many occasions, we only realise after many years that our children are not doing what they want to do. They are actually chasing the goals others have set for them. They only become aware much later that studying for a particular subject was not what they wanted. They did it because their parents told them to do it. They go through life without summing up the courage and determination to decide what they want.

The message from the trainer was clear: the thinking of parents towards their children must be appropriate. Her message was to love and nurture them rather than control and force them to live out the parent's dreams. To most of us, this is a difficult thing to do. Most of us are the product of our parents' thinking. We have been programmed to think exactly like our parents unless we have made a special effort not to. But, the whole world has changed.

My parents would always tell me that I needed to be in the science stream. I do not think any parent would quarrel with that kind of so called positive programming but if the programming overturns the child's natural desires and preferences, it would be very unfair to the child. If I had the talent to be a musician and wanted to be one, my parents certainly would have frowned on hearing my intention. Whenever my young children expressed a desire to become musicians, I would spring up to my years of programming and say: "You are going to be in sciences not in music; Do you get that clear?" My colleague Jeremy always says: "Influence them but don't force them. Let them live their lives." I certainly am learning now to change my thinking because I want my kids to develop their own Rainbows.

We think a safe job is secure because that was what we were told. Then we realise that the safe job is not the one that we wanted. Our preferences are really elsewhere. Rarely do we find the courage to make the switch. We continue in the safe job though we are not happy about it. The result is that we do our jobs in a half-hearted manner because it is not what we want to do. In the process of repeatedly doing the same things, we become used to what we are doing. If the people whose company we keep tolerate mediocre performance, we just become content with average performance. We become average and are happy with being average.

We are in this state simply because we were unclear about what we want. We think that a secure job is the only way to survive, and we are unable to change at the appropriate time.

Clear Goals

A valued Australian friend and former colleague, Lisa Henningham, once shared a lovely story with me. The foxes had a meeting to nominate one among them to catch a rabbit for dinner.

The nominated fox spotted a rabbit and commenced the chase. The rabbit was very fast. It ran with great ingenuity and speed. Though the fox pursued the rabbit using all of the skills available, the rabbit managed to escape. The foxes had a post-mortem meeting to analyse the race. They were sure the objectives of the chase could have been achieved if only the nominated fox had been more skillful. It was at that moment, the nominated fox remarked: "Before you start dishing out criticism, let me remind you about the rules of the chase. Let's get one thing clear. While I was running for my dinner, the rabbit was running for its life." Different goals, different focus, different levels of effort.

Do we know what we are running for in our lives? Are we clear about our goals? And are we ready to make the necessary changes to achieve our goals? How much effort are you willing to put in to achieve your goals? One key message that emerges out of all motivation work is that success is a result of the effort that you put in to achieve what you want. When you know what you want and you really want it very much, you go all out to get it.

Action

A clear focus should result in a specific results oriented action. Try giving work to people who are focused in what they want. They are excited about doing a job. Just look at the results. They may not be the most qualified people but they go out and learn and do everything that is needed to make the job a success. For those people without the focus, change can be worrisome. Look at middle aged professionals who have to change careers unexpectedly. They are very nervous about what the new situation will hold for them but yet they do know they are not happy with the current situation.

We become doctors, lawyers or government employees because our parents told us that it is the best thing for us. It is very impressive but deep down inside of us it is very suppressive because we are showcasing not ours but other people's goals. Our inner self tells us we desire something else. However, we decide that it is too late to change and it is not easy.

An action originates from a clear focus that includes three essential ingredients:

1. Prioritisation
2. Attitudes, and
3. Skills

Prioritisation

Here's an interesting story about one of my friends. My friend is a dentist. He chose to study medicine rather than follow his dreams because his parents wanted a doctor in the family. He gave up his dreams to satisfy his parents. Even though eastern cultures are changing, these cultures are more collectivist than western ones. The family's influence over individuals is still very significant though it is rapidly changing.

Although he ran a successful practice for over 20 years, he now wanted to do more. An extrovert, he always looked forward to doing voluntary work. Sundays were spent at free medical camps, much to the chagrin of his wife. Married with a beautiful wife and two lovely sons, life seemed very happy. However he didn't look very happy.

His job, he was so sure was not compatible with his preferences. He needed no Myers Briggs Type Indicator to tell him that.

Although he had a good lifestyle, he wanted to do what he liked to do. He liked to go out and meet people to make a difference to peoples' lives. The driving force was to do much more than what he was already doing. He now wanted to change his career and be courageous to pursue the goals he wanted to achieve. His desire to pursue a job in the life insurance industry required him to change the thinking that 'people cannot change careers in mid life'.

More importantly, he had to take the risk by taking action, to move from a shielded job to one that he likes but that was not necessarily secure. This move required him to prioritise his goals. He had to ensure his family commitments were met, especially the education of his children. Changing his profession for his personal satisfaction did not mean personal abdication.

Attitudes

Finally, at the age of 45 and after two years of preparation along with a positive attitude, he moved from dentistry to becoming a life insurance counsellor. Giving up a stable job might sound crazy; well, that is exactly what many people told him. He let his inner self guide him. The decision he took was practical and not rash. By still practicing dentistry once a week, he was able to secure some income while pursuing what he wanted. The remaining time he did what he wanted to do, helping people to plan their lives and take care of their families. Just three years into the business, he has done reasonably well though he had to work through the ranks.

His attitude demonstrated the fact that it is never too late to change and do what you want and make a contribution to society. The courage and conviction to pursue what he wanted must be lauded for he took the risk to follow his inner-self. While he listened to many, he made his own decisions. He took into account what others said but did not compromise his desire to satisfy his needs or accomplish his goals.

Skills

You have within you the ability to decide what you want. Rainbow Creators go out and learn the new skills required for change and for success. To them, learning is the means to achieving an end. My friend had to learn completely new skills of salesmanship, the insurance business, agency management and various other new things totally different from dentistry. He did not frown that he had to learn new skills at the age of 45 in the company of others about 20 years his junior. He fully realised the need to learn and to be competent in his new field. Learning the skills would help accelerate his efforts to rainbow creation.

Personal Experiences

My greatest satisfaction in my career comes from a decision I took about 20 years ago.

As a management development training specialist, I was aware that I was a good trainer and lecturer. However, I was also aware of the fact that learner retention was not as good as I hoped it would be. I reflected upon my school and university days. Some of my favourite teachers were more or less like me. They taught the subjects and left the responsibility of learning to the students. They motivated us to learn with interest.

Several decades ago, I attended participative training sessions and invested a huge amount of time to learn more about participative training methods. The session by Prof. Dr. Don Kirkpatrick opened up a new dimension for me. His use of humour and learner oriented activities aroused my learning curiosity. I also attended sessions by Dave Meier, Director of the Accelerated Learning Centre and Prof. Dr. Mel Silbermann, who pioneered the use of active learning tools. My experience forced me to reflect and analyse my own sessions. I was nervous about changing my training style because of my comfort zone that had been developed over the years. Yet, I began to attend sessions by other participative trainers such as Robert Pike of Creative Training Techniques International, and Prof. Dr. Thiagi at the University of Indiana, Bloomington. My enthusiasm led me to learn more about participative and creative training.

The reason for this enthusiasm was that these sessions placed the learner at the forefront. The goal was to translate learning into performance. Though I discovered that training is not the only solution to all performance problems, I discovered, to my surprise, that learning could be fun, easy and exciting. This insight changed my career dramatically. I began to focus on how to make learning fun for the learner and how to translate that learning into performance at the workplace, in an Asian context.

After nearly five years of research and practice, I summoned up courage in 1991 to overcome my fear and, with great trepidation, presented a session on how to make learning fun, in Kuala Lumpur. I was even more nervous because of the presence of Professor Thiagi and the presence of many senior training professionals such as Asma Abdullah, then Training Manager at Esso, in the audience. Though they were supportive, I was unsure of the response from the audience. To my surprise, the response from the audience was unbelievably positive. It boosted my confidence. My training practice went through a complete transformation. I redesigned all my materials to make my sessions learner-oriented and fun based.

Since then I have presented my session - The Magic of Making Learning FUN!! - to thousands of practitioners in many different countries. I had to overcome cynicism, skepticism and fierce criticism in the initial 12 months. It was not an easy task to get senior practitioners to understand that fun does not necessarily mean funny. Or that in fun training you do not have to be a clown. To get them to put the learner at the forefront and put the trainer behind was no easy task. It required a paradigm shift i.e. a major conceptual change, to get them to accept that fun training is also a professional way of helping people learn to perform at the workplace. They were nervous, as I had been, about changing what they had done for the past 20 or 30 years.

Today people write to me about the amazing results they have had with learner-oriented fun training sessions. Learners enjoy the sessions, they are able to transfer the learning to the workplace and they are excited about learning new ideas and skills. It is a great feeling when people write and tell me about the resounding success they have had with the fun training methods in their training sessions. To me, this great satisfaction that I have been able to influence fellow training professionals in a positive way is a result of the decision that I took several years ago to change my training style. This change has helped me as well as numerous other trainers in various countries to create our own Rainbows in our chosen profession.

Rainbow Creators have a clear focus and they are action oriented. They know what they want and they make the appropriate changes to flow in the direction of change to create their own Rainbow.

Are you ready for a change for the better?

Consider this: How about trying to become the BEST person you can be?

Remember what President Jimmy Carter said "We need to change with changing times but with unchanging principles."

"Change with changing times
but with
unchanging principles"
-Jimmy Carter

Reflections Three

List three things you have to do and three things you have to give up to achieve your potential - your purpose in life.

To do

To give up

Chapter Six:
Invoking your determination

....

"Try and fail, but don't fail to try."

-- Stephen Kaggura

Courage

The ultimate test of a person is not what he/she stands for in moments of luxury and joy, but where they stand at times of challenge, adversity and controversy.

Rainbow Creators always believe in themselves. They develop the ability to show courage when faced with adversity; they face change positively and influence others to change in a positive manner. Their goal is to make a positive contribution to the world they live in. They are physically and mentally prepared. This requires tremendous determination. People who are determined make it look so simple and make it happen by design with hard work.

It takes courage to change the way you have thought all your life. Again, after the change you may not succeed instantly.

Rainbow Creators, just like other people, face many hurdles but they are determined and this comes from persistence, work ethics, optimism – these are the keys they use to achieve what they set out to.

Persistence

If Asian leaders like Mahatma Gandhi (India), President Sukarno (Indonesia), Tuanku Abdul Rahman (Malaysia) or African leaders such as Nelson Mandela (South Africa) were not determined and persistent in their efforts to gain independence for the people in their countries, one billion people would not be independent today. President Nelson Mandela's singular determination to end apartheid resulted in freedom for millions of Africans. None of the freedom fighters achieved success instantly. They worked hard for years to overcome prejudice and hatred, sometimes at great personal sacrifice. President Nelson Mandela spent most of his life in prison. He could have easily given up but he persisted in his efforts to liberate his country from the indignity of slavery and apartheid.

Work Ethics

A journalist reportedly told the late great violinist, conductor, teacher and humanitarian Sir Yehudi Menuhin: "Sir, you are very lucky. God has given you a great talent." He replied: "Yes, if working 20 hours a day for the last 30 years is lucky, yes, I am very lucky." Isn't it true that the harder you work, the luckier you get?

It is funny but true that you only choose to work hard when you are persistent and determined to achieve what you want. We find the determination and persistence to overcome all the hurdles that are put in our way all the time. Zig Ziglar is fond of saying that we live in a world that is dominated by negativity. To succeed, he says, we need to be positive in everything that we do. In prosperity, it is easier to cope with the situation. It is in the midst of adversity that a person's real character emerges.

Determination is not about what you do when you have all the resources; it is about what you do when you have nothing but yourself.

OPTIMISM
- Seeing Problems as Opportunities

One of my friends was very busy with his dentistry work. He did not have much time for his wife and two sons. The family constantly argued with him about his absence. David Copperfield, the international magician, arrived in Kuala Lumpur in the early nineties, to perform his magic shows. My friend talked to me about his intention to take the family to the show. He wanted to purchase the most expensive seats costing $100 each. I was delighted about him taking his the family out. Within a few minutes, he said, "I hope David will make my wife and two kids disappear and then my problems will disappear too."

Though the comment was made in jest, I wondered how many of us actually hope that problems will simply fade away. Colleagues have inter-personal problems, married couples have difficulties and all of us have some form of difficulty. They do not disappear but, on the contrary, hinder us from going after our rainbows. It requires inner strength to work on problems; it calls for us to see every problem as a learning opportunity, for no problem is insurmountable when you have the will and determination.

Never Give Up

An incident that took place in the year 1991 remains fresh in my mind until today. There was a knock on the office door of our small office. The poster on the office door stated: 'No Salespeople'. Yet, a young man, hardly 21 years of age, peeped in through the door and said gently:

"My name is Chan, Sir and you are..."

"Palan," I responded.

"Sir, can I please come in and share a few ideas with you, just a few minutes of your time. This will probably be the best investment you have made in your life. "

I needed no further information to know that he was a life insurance salesperson. Not wanting to put him down but neither wanting to prolong the conversation, I said: "If it is life insurance, let me tell you, I have enough and I will not be interested. Good Day and Good Luck." I thought that was firm enough and that was the end of it.

That was not the end of it for him and he continued very quickly: "Wonderful Sir, that is pleasant news. I am always delighted to meet anyone who cares for the family and believes in life insurance. Wow! That is absolutely wonderful. May I just know one more thing, Sir? Which companies are you insured with, Sir?"

I thought this was now going a bit too far and really wanted the conversation to end quickly but politely. And, so I said: "Well, I am insured with AIA, one of world's best companies and my agent is a superstar Life Insurance agent. Further, I have coverage for one million. Would that be all right? Now, if you don't mind, I have an awful lot of work to do."

I was convinced it was over but not for him. He said: "Wunderba, fantastic, Sir. What a day? First I meet a person who cares for the family, has coverage for one million, insures with the same company as mine, AIA, and your agent is a great role model for people like me. Absolutely wonderful, Sir. But, Sir, how about giving a young person like me, who is just starting out now, a chance?"

This young man dumbfounded me. He overcame every single hurdle without any difficulty. His smile remained throughout his interaction with me. He never took any hurdle personally. The way he did it was so natural. Any customer would have been impressed with his determined and professional approach. I just said: "Come back in a year's time and if you are still in business, I assure you we will take a policy with you." He did, and I kept my word to do business with him.

Everybody has problems. The story of the great American President Abraham Lincoln is a clear testament that a person with determination and persistence cannot be stopped. Here is why:

Age	Result
21	failed in business
21	defeated in elections
24	failed in business
26	death of sweetheart
27	nervous breakdowns
34	lost Congress election
45	lost Senate election
47	failed Vice President Nomination
49	lost senatorial race
52	President of United States of America

Opportunities
are the
Little Windows
that show you
the path of success

Failures, problems and obstacles are common occurrences in life. It is not important how many times we fall. What is important is the ability to bounce back quickly. This is what separates the winners from the losers. Many friends tell me about how nice it is to speak at seminars or write about overcoming problems with a positive attitude. They complain bitterly that it is not that easy in real life.

Rainbow Creators do not look for excuses, they make things happen. Nothing is impossible if we work on the problems with determination and persistence. There is a saying "The difference between a successful person and others is not a lack of strength, not a lack of knowledge but rather a lack of will."

Nothing will replace determination and persistence as an ingredient for success. Talent, genius or education alone will not guarantee success. The world is full of talented people, geniuses and educated persons who did not succeed in life. Determination and persistence are critical for success.

Working at What You Believe In

My father's death was a devastating blow to my family and me. There was nothing to look forward to except problems. Within five years, my second sister also died. The untimely death of my father had left his business in shambles. My grandfather had died six years earlier. All the people who were bread winners had died and all of us, dependents were either in school or college.

My father's belief that knowledge will be the only sustainable competitive edge in the future had put every one of us through a college education. To him, knowledge was the key to the future. Now, it looked like none of us would even be able to complete our education, especially since were short of funds to pay the tuition fees to complete our education. If there was a perfect recipe for failure, we had all the ingredients for it. There was nothing to look forward to except problems. I had always wondered how we were going to survive this immense grief.

There were many stories that motivated me greatly. I read many of them. The stories of Henry Ford forgetting to put the reverse gear in his first car and Thomas Edison being sent away from school after three months because of his partial deafness helped me sustain my positive outlook towards life.

They say that these icons succeeded inspite of problems not because of the absence of them. Of course, I have my own stories, which today sound frightening because of the risks I took then. My enthusiasm to buy an estate and to export local products from Asia to the United States when I did not even have a single dollar in my pocket was a result of a desire to prove myself. Of course, I had supporters and mentors like my Uncle Maharaja Chettiar. They were willing to give me an opportunity without discouraging me or as the expression goes: throwing cold water in my face. They encouraged me and gave me opportunities, not charity.

Opportunities are the little windows that show you the path of success.

My mother was a hero to us. She had only completed primary education. She spoke only two languages: Tamil and Determination. In contrast to my father who was Westernised and modern in his outlook of life, my mother was the other extreme, very Indian and conservative. My father's death shattered her. She was only 45 years old and was suddenly faced with seven 'problems' in the shape of her seven children. The business was in shambles. Creditors were ready to eat us up.

There was enough goodwill and credibility for the family but there was no money. And, you need money to eat, study and survive. It looked like money was everything and you needed money to solve these problems.

My mother had never gone out of the house until then. Only 18 years old, I was not of much help. But, I saw my mother using the language of determination. She was depressed for three months. In a society where remarriage is unthinkable and unforgivable, she had to remain a widow. Archaic customs would not permit her to wear any more jewellery or lead a normal life. She would no longer be treated as she had been all this time by the society surrounding us. Her life for herself was over. Though committing "sati", the Indian practice of committing suicide after the husband's death, had long been discontinued among Indians, I learned from my own experience that it only applied to the physical. There was enough psychological 'sati' for women.

My mother could no longer *direct the wind but she could adjust the sails*. There was no way she could bring back my father but she could fulfill her dreams and my father's. She was determined to provide her seven children with the best education that was possible. She did not see us now as seven problems. She now saw us as seven challenges that she took upon herself. She was determined to succeed in her quest to give us the best education. She set out to work to achieve what she believed in i.e. a quality education for her children. She was our Rainbow Creator, on the way to creating her Rainbow and wanting all of us to work towards creating our own Rainbows.

Three months after my father's death, I began to see my mother very differently. She was still impatient, would raise her voice and expect us to communicate with her frequently. That was the way she had always been. However, now I saw a difference. She took over the leadership of the family and groomed me. I learned leadership and succession planning from my mother first. She was a practical teacher. The discussions were always positive and solutions oriented. The task was to resolve the problems and continue to pursue the Rainbow. As a student, I learned the Rainbow was VIBGYOR - violet, indigo, blue, green, yellow, orange and red. My mother taught me now how to pursue creating the VIBGYOR with vigour.

Charlie Flowers, a great Texan speaker, once said: "The best part of my life was spent with another man's wife." When the audience gasped, he added: "My father's wife." Certainly, my mom was my greatest inspiration and my best friend. She supported me in all of my efforts to create my own Rainbow. She did that for all her children. Her determination and persistence was the reason for me to develop into a young man driven with persistence and determination.

I remember the day in 1974 when I had gained admission to a private university. There was no money available to pay the fees. The travel and admission deadlines were drawing too near. Several approaches to friends, moneylenders and the banks were unsuccessful and led me nowhere. I walked back home nervous and depressed and was sitting out in the garden. My mind was wandering away into the darkness. I could see darkness spreading over my future.

I had just "given up" - I started to *justify the thought of helplessness* that if I continued to study in college to pursue my Rainbow, I may not be able to help my siblings because there would not be enough money for all of us to go to the university. That's it, I thought.

My mother had seen me come in, she walked by me. In a culture, where the hug and touch is not common, my mother broke a code of family life and sat down next to me. There was no conversation. There was no need for one. Both of us knew exactly the situation. Sometimes, as the Indian expression goes, only when it is dark enough, can you see clearly?

Aren't the stars clear at night? It is only in moments of sadness, that you begin to understand what happiness is. After a few minutes of a *loud silence*, my mother gave me her inherited jewellery, the jewellery my grandmother had given to her on her wedding day. She said: "Sell it and pay your fees. Stick to your travel plans. Get to college." The message was not to see the problem, but to look beyond it. It was a flash and the darkness disappeared. To me the night ended and the day had begun. I could now see my future. She was determined to make sure I created my own Rainbow too. Her happiness stemmed from helping me achieve mine. Mothers are Rainbow Creators for their children. That one decision that my mother and I made that night created my Rainbow. I was able to finish my Bachelor's, Master's and finally the Doctoral degrees.

To me, my mother personified determination, persistence and inspiration. My mother's support helped all of us, me and my siblings, to create our own Rainbows.

Reflections Four

Identity a person you have admired for his/her determination.

What do you think makes this person more determined than others?

Person admired

Qualities

Chapter Seven:

Never give up on yourself - Self Image & Self Suggestions

....

"No one can make you feel inferior without your permission."

- Eleanor Roosevelt

Faith in Yourself

The world is full of talented and educated people. Not all of them succeed in life, the problem is not their lack of talent or education but their self-belief. Very few have the confidence that they are capable of achieving much more than what they are doing currently. Most failures are due to a lack of confidence in their own abilities.

The first step in Creating Your Own Rainbow is about believing in yourself. Our accomplishments are critically associated with our self-image, our opinion of ourselves or the way we feel about ourselves. Computer specialists talk about the output from the computer depending on the information we put in. What goes in determines what comes out. Our self-image is the result of what we put into our minds. Our behaviour is a reflection of our self-image.

The way we think is largely influenced by the years of programming our mind. The influences have come from our families, peers and the company we keep. We have programmed our minds to act in a certain way - the do's and the don'ts have gone into our mind simply because we were the ones who put them in our minds. The way we act is, to a great degree, based on the way we feel about ourselves. Clearly, there are no restrictions other than the ones we put into our minds. Self¬ image is about having faith in yourself and reinforcing within yourself that you are capable of greater achievements. It is about developing a winning mindset and feeling good about you. Continuous self-suggestion that you are capable of Creating Your Own Rainbow improves the way you see yourself.

I remember one of the participants at a NTL, USA workshop making a comment about self esteem – 'why would you want to tell yourself something that you do not want others to tell you?'

There is a famous story on the golf circuit about the local golf professional who was competing with international professionals. At the end of the first day, the local golf pro was leading the pack. However, the local golf pro was very surprised with his winning performance. Local journalists were quick to point out that "self image should adjust itself within the next few days." True enough; the local golf pro went from leading the pack to finishing second last. We cannot perform beyond the boundaries of our self ¬image and the restrictions we impose on our capabilities.

As a young student debater, I used to be overwhelmed by the senior debaters. I did not have much faith in winning debating competitions because I suffered from an inferiority complex. I did not have the confidence to debate with the senior debaters. This influenced my performance. Defeat stared at me even before the competition began. I saw my weaknesses in my English, poor pronunciation and inexperience. To my speech coaches, Jesuit priests

Fathers Leonard Paul and George Maliekal; it was simply a lack of faith in me. Years later, one of my teachers and friends, psychiatrist Prof. Dr Peter Fernandez, would attribute this to a lack of self- esteem. He encouraged me to undergo a process of ego strengthening to see myself in a better way.

POSITIVE REINFORCEMENT

The self-image of a person is very fragile. It builds on success exponentially and breaks up on repeated failures. In my workshops, I tell the story of a butterfly. The butterfly is colourful, pretty but fragile. If you hold it in your palm and blow it gently, it flies into the air. Smash your palms and the butterfly is dead, leaving behind a greasy palm. Now you have to wash your palms with soap to get the grease off.

A person's self-image is very similar to a butterfly. In an environment of appreciation and reinforcement, the positive self-image of a person promotes a winning mindset. An environment of repeated disapproving criticism can smash the self-image of a person. You need a positive environment for the development of self-image.

No one develops it overnight. People work on building their self-image. Eleanor Roosevelt's words that no one can make you feel inferior without your permission is very true. What we are is a result of the internal programming of our minds. The intrinsic factors play a very important role in shaping our opinions about ourselves.

Many say that friends, parents and family programmed us to do what they wanted us to do. We are influenced by what people say from a very early age. Bill Cosby in his book "Kids Say the Darndest Things" writes about inviting five and six-year-old kids to his television show. He narrates incidents where their parents tell the kids what to do and say on the television programme. This is despite Cosby's advice to the parents to let their children be their natural selves. In one show, Cosby asks one of the kids: "Did your parents tell you what to do on the show? Did you have any training?" The young kid replies spontaneously: "Oh, yes! We had about six days training and my mom told me all the time - just don't make me look stupid." It was not about the kid but more about the mother.

We need to recognise the fact that people need to be themselves and to live their own lives. It is our responsibility to give ourselves, our kids, our colleagues and our friends' positive reinforcement that builds self-confidence.

We all learn very painfully that many other people do not believe in us. If this is added to the poor self-image of ourselves, we are what my mentor in the training field Professor Dr. Donald Kirkpatrick describes as being two strikes down even before the game has begun."

When I started our human resources consulting business from an answering service, there were enough people to discourage us. I remember a friend who with all good intentions remarked: 'quit and just get a decent job.'

We were clear in our minds about what we wanted to do. There was no doubt in our minds that we could help people learn effectively and help them develop into superior performers. Though many people gave us good reasons to quit from being self-employed, we were passionate about what we wanted to do. All the reasons - the recession, competition from international consulting firms and a host of other factors - did not dissuade us.

However, a few friends were ready to give us positive support. They did what they could to help rather than stop us from pursuing what we wanted. Today, after toiling for close to three decades, we can be proud that we are being recognised as a partner of choice for human resource development. The company is not the biggest nor does it employ thousands of people. That is not what we set out to do. Our goal was to help people learn and perform in a productive way and we are happy we were able to achieve our goals.

History repeats itself now and then. So, the same happened when I wanted to write my first book. There was much negativity. There were people who thought it was a waste of time. Some commented that my English was not good enough. The manuscript had too many spelling and grammatical errors. They said nobody would buy the book. It was just plain vanity. They were sure I was not yet ready to write a book. The best thing to do was to be just another trainer and forget about doing 'impossible' things like writing a book. Impossibility is more often a state of mind. And I was on a 'mission possible' trip.

As it turned out, most of the books did well. There were of course some that did not do well. That is life. Then, the same people who said it was an impossible task the first time were now saying that it is difficult to repeat the earlier success. This incident forced me to think about a situation few years ago, when I was losing confidence in my own ability until I received the support of two friends, Lisa Henningham, my former colleague from Australia and my college mate, Dr. Nat. They nudged me along, expressing confidence in my skills. What was needed was simply the self-belief that I could write a book. Of course, I needed to learn the skills but more importantly have faith in myself. After all, didn't Napoleon Hill say "If you can conceive it and you can believe in it, you can achieve it?"

It is important to have positive reinforcement. There is a need to be surrounded by positive people. They help build our self-confidence. My father always told me "Never delay what you want to do just because other people tell you it cannot be done." On reflection, I think I was lucky not to have allowed other people to make decisions for me when I was starting my business or writing my book. You need to make your own decisions and be personally responsible for them.

The popular story of Graham Laycock, a blind person and a successful physiotherapist enthuses people. He has travelled more than 150,000 kilometers in a few years sharing his message that people can achieve whatever they want so long as they really want it. His battle cry in life is "Those who say it cannot be done should not get in the way of those who are trying to do it."

Have you heard of Professor Muhammad Yunus, who started the Grameen Bank in Bangladesh? An economist, he was appalled with the banking system that was inaccessible to poor farmers. He created the Farmers Bank in 1994. The bank gives credit to poor farmers. The bank through the novel device of micro credit facility helped the disadvantaged. Poor traders and farmers whose income was less than one dollar benefitted a great deal. It gives the disadvantaged an opportunity and a better self-image. The Grameen bank experiment has been replicated in so many countries. And Professor Muhammad Yunus has won the Nobel Prize.

Neither Graham Laycock nor Professor Muhammad Yunus allowed lack of resources or their personal limitations restrict them from going after what they wanted. More than the money, the Grameen Bank experiment proved that even the desire to help build others' self-confidence can help others Create their Own Rainbows.

A Winning Mindset

I was intrigued to read about the famous sprinter, the late Flo Jo. She always set goals to beat her own records for she was sure that all that she needed to be a winner was to be a winner in her own mind first. Our self-image helps us succeed in certain ways. At the same time, it also rejects the many ways that could take us up to new levels of performance and success. Rainbow Creators have winning mindset that stems from positive self-image.

Feeling Good

Dr Maxwell Maltz, the author of the famous book *Psycho Cybernetics* describes the concept of self-image poignantly. As a plastic surgeon, he operated on people to make them better cosmetically - a nose job to make the nose higher and better looking, liposuction was to remove excess fat so that people could look slim. All his operations were performed to make people look good. There were before and after photographs. Dr Maltz was very surprised when his patients, on many occasions, did not detect any difference in their appearance. Even though the changes were substantial, they went away from the clinic upset. The 'before and after' photographs did not prove anything to them because they did not see the changes. Some of them went away happy after the operation only to express their disappointment after a few months.

"Do not let other's
perceptions of you
become true for you"
-Les Brown

Dr. Maltz had changed their external looks. He realised now that the people had been only operated on externally not within. Though they looked different, they did not feel different. Their self-image still was the same.

A friend qualified as an engineer, from a reputable American university. He accompanied me to a keynote presentation that I was to deliver for a large bank. There were about 300 executives attending the session. Throughout the session, I saw my friend sitting by himself. Not for a moment did he interact with anyone. After the session I asked him "How did you find the session?" He replied "I felt very inferior." He was probably more qualified than most people in that session but he had 'decided' he was inferior to them. I still remember telling him that it was his mindset. It took him a few months to work on his self-image. Today he is a confident and successful young man. He now lives in the United States and is very confident when competing with the best.

Your self-image can make you or break you. The way you see yourself will determine the way you see the world. The opportunities and the successes you have will be determined by the opinion you have of yourself more than what others will think of you.

People with severe disabilities have made it to the top. They have a high self-image. Nothing in this world will prevent them from going after their goals. They do not complain about their disabilities. On the other hand, they look for opportunities to succeed in life.

There are many that complain about the inequalities of life. True enough there are some serious problems arising from social inequalities. Dr Martin Luther King, Nelson Mandela and many others have tried to fight to end these inequalities.

For instance, the goal of affirmative action programmes is to try to end injustice to fellow human beings who are socially and economically deprived. But the point is, just because we are faced with inequalities does not mean we remain quiet. It is up to the person to develop his/her self¬ esteem in spite of these inequalities and strive to succeed in life. Martin Luther King did not choose to remain a preacher. Neither did Nelson Mandela choose to remain suppressed. They did not allow anyone else to tell them they were inferior. They fought to gain access to equal opportunity and to make a positive contribution to the world they live in. They looked at the possibilities of what they could do rather than suffer quietly.

While a positive self-image helps you develop into a Rainbow Creator, people with low self esteem put on a mask and end up as Rainbow Chasers. Here is a popular story shared by motivational speakers about a newly promoted executive who had a poor self-esteem. He found it very difficult to reconcile with the new office, position and responsibilities. The young executive on finding a visitor at his door, picked up the phone to demonstrate the importance of his position. He continued talking on the phone for a few minutes while the visitor waited. After putting down the phone, he asked the visitor "What can I do for you?" The visitor replied "I am here to fix your phone."

Low self-image comes from pretence or is influenced by it. It involves looking for a false sense of importance. People with low self-esteem are generally difficult to work with because most of them are stirrers. They get into a blame mode, criticising or blaming everyone else except looking at their own behaviour. The egocentric, dominant behaviour and the habit of talking about other people's deficiencies instead of their own come from a variety of factors such as negative self suggestions, upbringing and poor role models.

Dr Maxwell Maltz's book Psycho-Cybernetics had a profound influence on me. I grew up in a multicultural environment and this offered enough opportunities for me to recognise the effect of prejudices and stereotypes. I was very conscious of the colour of my complexion as I had personally experienced much discrimination. I had lost job opportunities. People had not wanted to sit next to me in buses. There were times when I retreated into my shell because of the fear of rejection. Such beliefs created low self esteem but I realised that this does not only come from the outside but can also emerge from within ourselves.

A friend negated my racial stereotypes. The friend was Fern, Professor Don Kirkpatrick's wife. I was a very young person when I met Fern. The conversation was pleasant but I was very nervous for it was the first time I had met a 'white' lady. She made me feel very comfortable and at the end of the conversation she planted a kiss on my cheek and said "Palan, you are wonderful, you are also one of us, do visit us." It was then that I realised that though stereotypes and prejudices exist in the harsh world out there sometimes the prejudice is actually more in our minds rather than in the minds of the people. We allow a few incidents to become the truth for us. Remember what Les Brown, the motivational speaker said: "do not let others' label of you become a reality for you."

Rainbow Creators work on their self-image. Many years ago, I worked with Elsie Chong, a dynamic lady. She once told me "Palan, I am not your superior to comment on your dressing, but let me tell you. It is good to dress well for it makes you feel good. If you do not look after yourself, how can you look after other people?" Rainbow Creators feel good about themselves. It is important that we begin to have faith in ourselves.

SELF SUGGESTIONS

Twenty-five years ago I entered a national school debate. After several grueling rounds, I was in the finals. I was really very nervous. I went up to my father and said "Dad, do you think I can win this debate? I am really very worried, dad." He looked at me and said "Son, it is just that you are very much like your mother. If your mother had not been so worried, you would have been one year older." It was a comment made in jest but I still remember what he said to me afterwards.

"Son, prepare your best and more than that, believe you can win it. Visualise yourself receiving the prize." All that my father was trying to get me to do was to believe in myself.

W. Clement Stone says *autosuggestions* have a powerful influence on the subconscious mind. It is important to remember that our conscious mind has the ability to accept and reject. The subconscious mind only accepts, it makes no distinction about the input. If the mind is fed with thoughts of doubt, fear, hate, blame and prejudice, the *autosuggestions* mechanism will activate and translate those thoughts into action. The subconscious is the database. The difference between the subconscious and the conscious is simple. While the subconscious is like a car, the conscious is like the driver. The power is in the car but the driver has the control.

The subconscious mind is also like a farm. It does not matter what you grow. It is neutral and has no specific preferences. If you plant good seeds, you have a good crop. If the seed is of poor quality, the crop is going to be poor. The human mind is very similar.

A successful life insurance professional and motivational speaker, my friend Benny Ong, once shared this lovely story with me. A young man who worked for him approached Benny and said "Boss, I am seeing this customer, do you think I can close the sale or not? I don't think I can close this sale, lah. What do you think?" Benny had no hesitation in replying "I also think you can't close the sale, lah."

Of course, the young man had programmed himself to fail. If he had used the power of autosuggestion and reinforced the words "I can do it" and visualised it positively, the results certainly could been different. The feeling of happiness that accompanies a successful sale can be lived out in your mind. When we reinforce the successful feeling time and again, you develop a winning mindset, which prompts you towards the path of success.

One of my valued colleagues is a brilliant artist and a professional designer. However, she had deep rooted fears about her ability to speak. It was further compounded by her upbringing and vernacular education. All these factors contributed to her becoming an introvert and shy person. She programmed this upbringing of introversion as inferiority to others. The deep inferiority complex resulted in her suggesting to herself, "I can't do it."

After, she attended a session that helped her work on her fears; she grew out of her self imposed shell. She has used the tools of autosuggestion and visualisation very well. Today, she is a much more confident person though she still continues to work on her self-doubts.

Positive auto-suggestions can programme both your subconscious and conscious mind. It can play a very important role in you creating your own Rainbow. Change what you put into your mind and the results are dramatically different. When a person repeats the autosuggestions long enough, it sinks into the subconscious and becomes reality. Add the power of visualisation, when you create a positive picture in your mind of what you want to achieve, to auto suggestions. You will be amazed with the results.

Every July, we organise an event - the Regional Trainers Meet Trainers (TMT) Convention (now known as the Asia HRD Congress) at Kuala Lumpur. It is one of the largest HRD events in Asia. We fund and organise it ourselves. We usually worry intensely about whether we are going to get enough participants to attend the event. Our goal is to make it a better event every year. It is a tough task. Some years ago we came across the idea of auto suggestions and visualisation. We constantly suggest to ourselves:

We are going to make it,
We can do it,
We are going to be WINNERS and
We are the BEST!

There is a celebration every time we reach a milestone. We cut a cake or we sing a song to celebrate achieving the milestone. We do not say "How are we going to get another 500?" On the contrary we say "25 a day for the next 20 days." We visualise the picture of registering 1000 people and the crowds milling at the Convention floor.

The purpose is to reinforce in our subconscious that we can do it. Positive autosuggestions and visualisations make you internally driven. It is a good practice to be internally driven rather than externally driven. When you are internally driven, you are connected with the purpose of your life. The moment you are solely externally driven, you go about life in a mechanical way.

Start to focus on what you want to achieve in life. Remember the simple principles of autosuggestions and visualisation. Let us not look into the past all the time and use that as a benchmark. If we did that, it is very unlikely we would reach our destination successfully. We will hit obstacles all the way through. On the contrary, grab the bull by the horns as they say, look clearly into the future and chart your path to your destination. Don't think about how boring and long the journey is going to be. On the contrary, think of it as a pleasant journey and life will be a lot better. Analysing without learning from past failures and dwelling on them forever without moving forward will only mean more setbacks. Analysis without action is paralysis. Grab the controls of your life and believe you can succeed, and you will have the drive to be where you want to go. Act NOW for the present moment is all that you have.

The rainbow is one of nature's wonders. You can simulate wonders in your life too. You can create your own rainbow and become one of your family's, community's and humanity's wonders. The power of autosuggestions and visualisation will help you achieve your goals.

Many years ago, while reading the SUCCESS magazine, I came across this poem which was found on the cell walls of two prisoners on the death row.

The Person in the Mirror

When you get what you want in your struggle for self,
And the world makes you Emperor for a day,
Then go to the mirror and look at yourself,
And see what the Person in the mirror has to say,
For it isn't a person's father, mother or spouse,
Whose judgment the person must pass,
The fellow whose verdict counts most in life,
Is the person staring back from the mirror?
The fellow in the mirror is the person to please,
Never mind the rest,
For the person is with you up to the end,
And you have passed your most dangerous, difficult test,
If the person in the mirror is your friend,
You can fool the whole world down the path way of years,
And get pats on your back as you pass,
But your final reward will be heartache and tears,
If you have cheated the person in the mirror.

Reflections Five

What are the factors that:

Promote your self-esteem

Lower your self-esteem

Chapter Eight:

Believe in Desire & Enthusiasm

....

"You have to dream before your dream can become true."

- Abdul Kalam, President of India

A Fuel for Success

The desire to succeed, win and the enthusiasm to try are the things that endure. These qualities are more important than the events that occur. Rainbow Creators have these qualities. Their desire and unlimited enthusiasm is the fuel that powers them towards success – what they want to achieve.

Secret to Success

The story of a young man asking Socrates the secret of success has been made popular by motivational speakers. To answer the question, Socrates takes the young man for a walk down the river. After a short while, he persuades the young man to have a swim in the river. When they get into the river, Socrates grabs the young man and ducks him into the river. The young man struggles to get out of the river but Socrates manages to keep him there for a short while. When Socrates pulls him out of the water and asks him, "What did you want when you were in the water?" The young man replies "Air." Socrates is reported to have then said "That is the secret to success. When you desire success as badly as you want the air, then you will succeed. "

My friend Michael Jenkins, who trains executives on the art of public speaking, talks of the burning desire or the fire in the belly to succeed as a public speaker. When you have a burning desire and you are enthusiastic about getting your message across to the audience, then your task becomes a delight.

Michelangelo, the famous Italian sculptor and painting master, worked extremely hard and this was attributed to his enthusiasm. He was often quoted as saying "If only people knew how hard I had to work to acquire my skills, it would not seem wonderful at all".

Unlimited Enthusiasm

The desire to transform our HRD business into an international one led us to get into the software business. We developed and named the product HRDPower, the internationally acclaimed competency based HRD software that our company now owns. I still remember the day we made the decision to invest in the development of HRDPower. The economy in the region had slowed down and while we were eager to invest in a software product, we were terrified of venturing into new territory in an uncertain time. Family and professional colleagues advised us to "go slow:" The uncertainty caused by the economic upheaval was a cause for concern.

It was past seven in the evening. Only Jeremy, my colleague and I remained in the office. It had been a long day. Jeremy shared with me his views and said "Well, what do you think?" Instead of replying to his question, I asked another question "Jeremy, what do you think?" He did not hesitate for a moment but his reply reverberated through the office.

He said "Palan, I have told you about the opportunities. You have to decide but if you ask me, I am 63 years old and I am very excited." I did not pause for another moment. We went ahead and allocated the resources. Jeremy's enthusiasm and desire to go global sparked off my own desire and enthusiasm. It was then that the words of Charles Schwab echoed in my ears "People can succeed at almost anything for which they have unlimited enthusiasm." Desire and enthusiasm is the catalyst that causes possibilities to grow into realities.

Everything that we have done has not been without problems but we have not regretted the move. It has helped us take the business into a growth area besides making it a truly global one. I am sure that when we reflect upon our actions in the future, it might appear as one of the best decisions we made for the company.

Watering Your Seeds

Paul Hanna, one of Australia's foremost motivational speakers, says that to build desire and enthusiasm you have to regularly 'water your seeds.' People start getting excited when they first decide to buy a new car or house, or begin planning to take a vacation. You see an advertisement that promotes the new model of a car. You've always wanted to have such a car and you start to think, "Maybe I deserve the car." The seed is planted. You see advertisements and articles about the car in the motoring section of your newspaper. You start to seriously consider investing in the car. On your way back home, you visit the dealer to see the car. You have not only planted the seed but you are also regularly watering the seed. The planted seed does not grow into a beautiful flower the next day. You need to look after it and give it time to grow.

Unfortunately, very few people take this approach. They try various short cut methods like gambling and lotteries to achieve success overnight. Rainbow Chasers spend their time forever chasing instant riches that have always eluded them.

While your self-image will determine whether you will become 'the best person you can be.' All of us have two choices when it comes to changing how we feel about ourselves. We can sit by idly waiting for the angel to come and change things for us or we can make a difference by taking control of our life. Taking control of our life means desire and enthusiasm with which we can grow into Rainbow Creators.

QUALIFICATIONS

Some friends tell me that they do know what they want. They have the desire and enthusiasm but the problem is everyone else tells them that they are not qualified. They do not have the entry qualifications, the money or the support to do what they want to do. They claim that more than desire and enthusiasm, it is the qualification that matters most.

I am convinced that the moment you talk about the reasons why you cannot pursue your goals instead of looking at ways of achieving them, desire and enthusiasm are absent. Talking about qualifications, I am reminded what the late Sony Bono, the multi-talented former husband of famous singer Cher, had to say "What is being qualified? What have I qualified for in my life? I haven't been qualified to be a Mayor. I am not qualified to be a successful songwriter. I am not qualified to be a hit TV producer. Nor am I qualified to be a successful businessman or a Congressman. And so, I don't know what qualified means. I think people get too hung up on qualifications in a way, you know." I think Sony Bono's words make a lot of sense. Very often it is all in our mind. If we needed something real bad, we will be determined enough to learn the skills to ensure we succeed. After all, didn't Sony Bono learn how to be a songwriter, mayor and congressman?

Do not let the lack of qualification, money or support stop you from pursuing your goals. Most great people more than their qualifications had the desire and enthusiasm to make a contribution and pursue their lifetime goals. Remember that Thomas Edison pursued his goal but he failed a thousand times before he perfected the electric bulb.

I was not qualified to become a trainer or writer before I embarked on my career. It was sheer desire and contagious enthusiasm that sparked me on my career route as a trainer, writer, or technopreneur. I learned what I needed to achieve my goals.

VISUALISATION

Rainbow Creators visualise and mentally rehearse to build desire and enthusiasm. The more you remind yourself of what you want and the more you intensify your desire to achieve it, you will become more comfortable with what you want. Visualisation helps you remain focussed in creating your Rainbow.

I always try to picture moments of joy in the past, like the time when I secured a big contract. It is great to recreate the successful moments. Excitement and moments of joy usher in a good feeling. I enjoy every moment of it.

"The most pathetic person
in the world
is someone who has sight,
but has no vision"
-Helen Keller

Sport stars know the power of recollecting the moments of old glory. Can you think of something in your life that really motivated you? Can you think of an event in your life in which the desire in you to produce your very best form outweighed your qualifications? Do you recollect how happy you felt? I am sure you would like to relive those moments once again. Phil McGraw asks his participants to think about the defining moment of their lives.

I have read the achievements of many great people including the great Roman, Julius Caesar. He shared his desire and enthusiasm to put Rome on the world map. Romans, in turn, were excited with Julius Caesar's vision.

People often ask me if enthusiasm and desire to achieve your goals is enough for success. What can they do for your success? My answer is very simple; they can do everything for you that a lack of desire and enthusiasm cannot.

Every time I get a writer's block, I picture the success I had with my first book. I recollect the joy of reading a one-page review of my book that featured prominently in the nation's foremost English daily. I visualise the feedback from the readers. The feeling that I had been able to assist others helps me to rekindle my enthusiasm and overcome the writer's block.

Rainbow Creators are those who are in charge of things. They do not let events prevent them from achieving their goals. They work enthusiastically for what they believe in.

Excitement

The interaction I have had with a telemarketing colleague is a unique one when I visited the telemarketing department. The moment I entered into the telemarketing room, I was greeted with an infectious greeting "Good Morning." Feeling very welcome, but recognising the tough business climate, I asked:

"How is it going?" "Fantastic!" she replied.

"How many calls do you plan to make today?"

"Just one hundred as every day"

"And, how many have you made today?"

"70 more to go."

"Any luck as yet today?"

"Well, every one of the remaining 70 calls is a strong possibility".

"You seemed so excited about phoning people.

How long have you been telemarketing?" "For the last 15 years."

"Aren't you bored? How do you feel when a person slams the phone on you?"

"Bored! You must be joking; this is my life, sir. If a person slams the phone on me, I do not take it personal. They have just missed out on a wonderful opportunity. I am not going to let a person who bangs the phone on me to control my life. I do not want to be externally driven. I wish to be internally driven; I want to be in control of myself.

Reverend Robert Schuller's words made sense – "There are tough times but remember tough times do not last, tough people do." You will always miss 100 percent of the shots you don't take in the soccer field. It was certainly a lecture but I left the room with a good feeling. Despite telemarketing in a tough economic environment, her desire to succeed and unlimited enthusiasm were clearly visible.

'Today well lived makes every yesterday a dream of happiness, and every tomorrow a vision of hope." Enthusiasm can help us be happy.

Consider the story of a 100-year old lady celebrating her birthday. There were many guests and journalists attending the birthday party. As the birthday cake was about to be cut, the old lady was completely caught up with the excitement of the day. Just then, the journalist approached her and asked "Do you have any children?" "Not yet," she responded without any hesitation.

It is important to be excited about what life offers us rather than look at it in a pessimistic way.

DESIRE TO OUT BEAT YOURSELF

When we organise large conferences, we find it to be a tough job. It is really difficult because we do everything by ourselves. The participation fee is kept very low to make it affordable for many people to attend the event. This means we cannot hire too many people. Productivity is a central issue. Everybody on the team needs to do everything.

The full-time and part-time staffs are overwhelmed with work. We meet every evening to share ideas. The goal is how to maximise customer satisfaction. Everyone is really charged up to provide the best. Every team member is enthusiastic about their roles. As the CEO of Success Factors, USA says, there is no place for jerks here. At the end of the meeting, we hold hands to motivate ourselves with a slogan. We chant our slogan "We want to be the BEST, B for Better, E for Excellence, S for Superb and T for Terrific." We create the enthusiasm and the desire to be better than what we have been. It is also in a sense, auto-suggestions to be our best.

Look within YOU

Friends ask if we have problems. Of course, we have problems. The goal is to succeed in spite of problems, not in the absence of them. The stress is sometimes unbearable but we remind ourselves that we are Rainbow Creators. We need to manage the stress with some of the techniques that are available to us today - music, prayers, meditation, good laughter and moving away from a negative frame of mind to a positive one.

Madan Kataria talks about the power of laughter and the need to laugh for no reason. A laughter environment creates a productive workplace.

Having faith in yourself and the using the power of autosuggestions that you can succeed are important. There are no short cuts to success. Plant a seed of desire, water it regularly with your self-esteem and stay focused on your goals. Rainbow Creators do that all the time. Intense desire and contagious enthusiasm is a powerful catalyst to Creating Your Rainbow.

There are people who look 'outside' for solutions to their challenges, when the answer actually lies within them.

Remember what Ralph Waldo Emerson said "What lies behind us and what lies before us are tiny matters compared to what lies within us."

"What lies behind us
and what lies before us
are tiny matters compared to
what lies within us."
- Ralph Waldo Emerson

Reflections Six

How can we promote desire and enthusiasm?

In ourselves

In others

Chapter Nine:
Optimal Leadership & Adventure

....

"Seek truth from facts."

-- Deng Xiaoping

INFLUENCING PEOPLE

Leaders not only have the desire to look at the exception; they also have the desire, enthusiasm and a spirit of adventure to become exceptional. They aim to be the best as well as influence others to aim for their best.

Leadership is about influencing people and getting results. The ability to get people to do things willingly is an important pre-requisite for successful leadership. Leaders are Rainbow Creators who help others create their own Rainbows. It is about motivating people to use their initiative to get things done in the right way and at the right time. It is not about getting individuals to become blind followers. My colleague Ramley is fond of quoting General Eisenhower "You do not hit people on their heads to get things done." And Ramley adds "Not even in the army".

Treating people with Care

The leader determines the speed of the pack. Leadership is about motivating people with whom you work and in creating willing followers. Willing followers are those who are enthusiastic about creating a Rainbow for themselves and others. It is not giving up your identity and becoming a cheer group. Good leaders treat people with care. They do not put down others even if it means giving straight feedback.

I know of a person who picks a quarrel with everyone he works with. He later regrets it but by then nobody wants to work with him. They now avoid him because it is too stressful to work with him. He came by to discuss his situation with me. My Asian upbringing did not allow me to tell him straight, what I really wanted but I shared the following popular story with him.

The story of a manager scolding the staff only to regret it later is a story we can learn from. Apparently, the manager regretted the use of offensive words. To make things up, the manager went to the priest to make a confession and seek forgiveness. The priest told the manager to go to the park with a bag of feathers and drop them in the centre of the park. The manager did as he was told and went back to see the priest. Now, the priest told him to go back to the park and collect the feathers. The manager was shocked and blurted "The feathers would have all been blown away, I can't collect them now." The priest now responded "The same thing is true with your words. You dropped them like the feathers easily but you cannot retrieve them. Take care when using your words.

Dealing With People

Successful leaders inspire people to develop their self-image and help them remain focused in their goals. They are emotionally intelligent. Emotional Intelligence is nothing more than bringing emotion to your intelligence. Leaders high in emotional intelligence are not necessarily nice; they are assertive and they express their emotions congruently. The only difference is that they do it appropriately. They do not put people down by hitting at their self esteem. Remember the butterfly story when we talked about self-esteem. Do you promote or destroy self-esteem of others? People are valuable companions and we need them to help us and strike a WIN: WIN relationship.

This is why corporate leaders often choose managers who are more capable of dealing with people rather than any other ability.

Thinking Positively About People

Leadership is much more than charisma. It is about a positive people orientation.

Are you positive about people? Just reflect upon people who have irritated you in recent times. How much negativity have you generated towards them? For every action, there is a reaction. You would have possibly attracted similar negativity from the other person. There is no such thing as one person being solely responsible. It takes two to tango.

Some of the experiences I have had with one of my siblings were painful. Most of the time, the family had communicated their displeasure for the sibling's lack of direction in life or self-management. There were always problems and the entire family tried to be supportive, I couldn't avoid being negative at times. The negativity did not solve any issues. We learned with great pain that we had to respond positively and to let the sibling be responsible and take personal accountability.

Leaders make people feel comfortable rather than tense.

The Power of Smiles

My schoolteacher, Mrs. Smith, would always say "Think of people in positive terms and always remember to smile. When you do that, you will set miles of smiles!" Politicians who smile garner more support than there who don't. We are all capable of smiling in our way. People treat you better than they normally do when you give them a smile.

The more you smile, the more natural it becomes and you become very comfortable with it. Leaders relate to people and all of us can develop our own charisma in our own ways to influence people in positive ways.

I can only think Singapore Airlines, a great airline to fly. Believe me, I have flown so many airlines and Singapore Airlines stands heads and shoulders over others. It is a great way to fly with them. The smile is authentic and backed by the genuine willingness to serve; and the *possibility thinking*, their service levels accelerate above others. There may be shortcomings but the goodwill far outweighs the shortcomings.

Smile is a deliberate act of decency.

Deliberate acts of decency

Effective leaders use decencies to build great workforces with one gesture at a time. Steve Harrison writing in the HR magazine talks about examples of best practices that he calls as decencies. You can mould a company culture by adopting small decencies. In my own experience, I have either experienced some of these decencies with the people who I worked for or have tried them out. It is about the way leaders choose to behave – the actions leaders embrace – everyday, especially during the quiet moments when we think no one is watching. Some of them are:

1. Be sure that nothing important or creative is perceived as the leader's idea,
2. Write personal notes to employees and customers,
3. Walk an employee or a customer to the door,
4. Always greet people in a sincere way,
5. Make as many allies as you can within the organisation all the time,
6. Talk about disagreements in private personally and try to resolve them or at least agree to disagree,
7. Let every employee have a sense of ownership – give them a business card,
8. Mix with people from other departments,
9. Praise in public and reprimand in private,
10. Be accessible to people.

They do not seem very difficult, do they?

Decencies need to be *actionable, tangible, practical, affordable, replicable and sustainable.* Once leaders practice the decencies regularly, employees start taking it seriously. Pretty soon, if you are honest as a leader, you would have developed a new organisational culture.

Character

Leadership is about character. Good character is a combination of honesty, selflessness, understanding, beliefs, courage, loyalty and respect. Phillip Brooks says that character may be manifested in the great moments, but it is made in the small ones.

The popular story of Shannon Miller's gold medal winning performance at the 1996 Summer Olympics is an awesome one. She won with a near-perfect balance beam performance. It was a great moment for her and her country. She was the first American to win both an individual and a team gold medal in a fully attended Olympics contest. What people did not realise was the fact that Miller's big moment was the climax of many smaller ones. Prior to that winning performance, she had spent more than 20,000 hours in practice under the mentoring of her leader, father and coach. She arrived at the gym by six in the morning to work out for about four hours. She returned again at four in the afternoon to work out another four hours. This she did for six days a week. She also managed to go to school and continue with the studies. Her father said "The people see the competition but we see four routines that we have been training daily for four years." It was her father's leadership that led her to success.

Jim Kirkpatrick shared with me the story of Dutch mountaineer Katja Staartjes, Her story was similar to Shannon Miller. Years of practice and respect for the mountain were what got her to the peak of Mount Everest. It was her leadership that got her and colleagues up and back safely.

Leaders do not allow their people to be discouraged if it seems the accomplishments are not much. They encourage and support people minute by minute and day by day which eventually add up to large accomplishments. They display a leadership character.

Remember the saying:

When wealth is lost, nothing is lost.

When health is lost, something is lost.

When character is lost, everything is lost.

Exemplary Leadership Practices

Kouzes and Posner talk about the five essential practices for exemplary leadership:

1. Modeling the Way
2. Inspiring a Shared Vision
3. Challenging the Process
4. Enabling Others to Act
5. Encouraging the Heart

Leadership is also about being a model for others. Unless you are a Rainbow Creator, you cannot inspire other people to create their Rainbows. It is about setting the right example and displaying initiative, which is what individuals need for success.

Let me relate to you the story of a famous Indian King who wanted to give away his only daughter in marriage to the bravest man in his kingdom. He arranged for all the young men to come to the palace grounds to demonstrate their bravery. On their arrival, he set out the terms. The young men were required to swim between the two banks of the river near the palace. The only problem was that the river was infested with crocodiles. As the young men discussed the situation, suddenly one of them was seen furiously swimming across to get to the other bank of the river. The King was delighted and ran up to the young man and said "Bravo, young man. Well done! Tell me the secrets of your bravery. The young man, in an agitated tone, said "Move away, king. Let me go and catch the person who pushed me into the river first."

It was neither initiative nor a role model that motivated the young man to swim but an external force, the fear of survival. How many times have we been 'pushed' by external forces rather than by 'internal drives?' It is an internal drive that sets apart great leaders from ordinary people. Leaders inspire their followers with their passion. Mahatma Gandhi gave the gift of political freedom from the British to the Indian people. Martin Luther King inspired his people with his dream of a free America.

Leadership is about challenging the process, making it possible for people to deliver results and finally touching the heart. Konrad Adenauer, the German Chancellor, remarked that though we all live under the same sky, we don't have the same horizons. Leaders are able to visualise what others are not able to. They share and inspire the others with their vision.

Lee Kuan Yew, the visionary Singaporean leader led his people to believe that they can be a successful nation provided they are ready to work. Today, Singapore is a success story and a role model for other nations.

Leaders are guides

Mothers are great leaders. Let me share the story of a young teenager who got upset with his mother and shouted at her "I hate you! I hate you!"

He ran to the valley and shouted the same words. He was shocked to hear the echo "I hate you, I hate you". Terrified, he ran to his mother and explained what had happened. The mother smiled and asked her son to run back to the valley and shout "I love you, I love you."

This time around, the young teenager heard the echo "I love you."

The mother guided the young teenager to understand love. She provided the leadership. Leaders guide the followers through a careful and caring process of coaching and mentoring, helping them move towards their Rainbow.

Leadership Behaviours

Stephen Covey, in his book The 7 Habits of Highly Effective Families, describes the leadership roles for the family, the four basic universal needs and how they relate to the four unique human gifts. He stresses the need for the family to laugh and have fun. As a leader in your family, in your work area and in your community, you have a responsibility to exercise effective leadership behaviours if you wish to be a role model. The role model he proposes is one of four needs requiring four roles to deliver the four gifts to the family.

Need	4 roles	Gifts
To learn	Teaching	Imagination
To live	Organising	Independent Will
To love	Mentoring	Self-Awareness
To leave a legacy	Modelling	Conscience

Adventure

Leaders are adventurers; they dare to dream and venture into the world of possibilities and push the limits of impossibility. You do not have to be a rich man, politician or a corporate manager to be a leader. All that you require is the willingness to lead your people, have courage to work hard and demonstrate the leadership practices. There is a saying that if you have the courage to begin, you will have the courage to finish.

Risks

You can't have an adventure without risks. Climbing Mount Everest is an adventure but it is also full of risks. Thousands attempt to climb the world's highest peak every year. Several expeditions scale Mount Everest every year but very few make it. The ones, who make it respect nature, follow the experience of earlier expeditions. Rainbow Creators want to be on top of the world, they take risks but they listen too, they challenge the process yet manage the risks for success. Creating Your Own Rainbow is all about adventure and taking risks.

Success involves making calculated risks. Success is most of the time a function of consistent common sense. It is not genius all the time. Common sense is the ability to remain objective in a difficult situation. It is about seeing things in a very simple and practical way.

Risk taking does not mean gambling. Risk takers are not gamblers. A risk taker builds a casino while a gambler plays poker in the casino. The person who never takes risks avoids making mistakes but neither does the person achieve anything. If you do not risk anything, then you risk losing everything.

"A ship in the harbour
is indeed safe
but that is not
what ships are built for."

There are people who are afraid to start a business because they may lose money. Some others do not wish to speak in public because their language is not good enough. They figure that by not doing anything they can get by. That is precisely what they do - get by, for their biggest mistake is doing nothing. The determination to travel on the road less travelled marks the difference between excellent performance and mediocrity.

The following motivational poster sums it up all:

"A ship in the harbour is indeed safe but that is not what ships are built for."

Let me narrate the popular story about a farmer. This farmer who had not planted anything is a good example of one who did not want to take any risk at all. On asked why he had not planted, he replied

"I was afraid it would not rain."

"Did you at least plant corn?"

"Oh, no! I was afraid the insects would eat it."

"What did you plant?"

"Nothing, I just played it safe."

Many opportunities are lost because of people's fear. They do not want to take risks or be adventurous. In the mid¬ eighties, when Malaysia was experiencing a difficult economic recession, we had to search for new markets.

The situation required us to travel out of the country. I was conducting a training session on the island of Labuan in East Malaysia. After I had finished my session, I was tempted to go to Brunei, the oil rich kingdom that was only a few minutes away from Labuan. These days, Labuan is a very well developed financial centre but at that time it was really a small town.

My friend Jamaluddin Zainal, then the Training Manager of Sabah Gas, suggested that I take the ferry to Brunei, as that would be the cheapest option. Flights were only available on selected days from Kota Kinabalu. I arrived at the port-terminal. There was no sign of ferries but the sign "To Brunei" was visible. When I asked where the tickets could be bought, the answer was "on the ferry". I followed the queue. Eventually we were guided on to a small boat not a ferry. The boat accommodated about 25 passengers. A small motor powered the boat. The ride was unbelievably cheap, about US$5 for the 45-minute journey. As the boat made its way into the high seas, I experienced some of the most frightening moments of my life. Every time the boat hit a wave, it looked like we would go under the sea. Eventually after a scary but an unforgettable forty-five minute journey, we arrived at breathtaking Bandar Seri Begawan, the capital of Brunei Negara Darussalam.

The customer visits in Brunei were fine. Just as I was about to take the flight back to Kuala Lumpur, a customer asked me the question that I hoped he would not ask "How did you get here? Did you take the flight from Singapore or Kota Kinabalu?" I decided to be honest and replied that I had taken the boat from Labuan. He smiled and said "That would have been a great experience. We call them 'superman' boats not because they are not really safe, but because they are a real adventure."

You can't explain adventure; you need to experience it - the feeling and your response to it. In the context of leading my organisation, I had to take the risk of going out of the country in search of new markets. To me the Brunei trip was great adventure and a very successful one.

Leadership and adventure is all about seeking out to achieve the impossible but it does not mean taking unrealistic and unsafe risks. My father would always say "Never compromise on three things Health, Safety and Education."

Nevertheless, that journey was a memorable and adventurous one. It was a bold decision but the investment of time and money paid off as we survived the recession with that contract.

Again, another incident that I have shared before and like to share again is one that made a huge difference to me. About two years ago, I embarked on my writing career with great support from my friend, Dr. Nat. I did not have the confidence. It was Nat who told me to practise what I preached - you could achieve what you want so long as you desire it. I discussed it with my wife who thought it was a great idea. My creative designer Khiem was very supportive. Khamsiah, my colleague for over nine years, shared my excitement. However, there were other people who gave me very good reasons not to write the book. I was just about to give up when I realised that I was allowing other people to make a decision for me, whether I should venture into the world of writing or not. Nat was a powerful influence and it was he who was very clear that the decision had to be mine whether to venture into the world of writing or not.

Risk taking is part of the process of creating your own rainbow. I decided to take a risk of investing my time and effort in writing a book. The experience was a great adventure. I was now able to share my experiences with other fellow professionals. Today, I don't regret a single moment. The book helped me create my own rainbow and helped other people create their own for they could now learn from the sharing. They did not have to learn through trial and error as I had done. The book *The Magic of Making Training FUN!!* helped show there are far more effective ways to train people. It was very satisfying when people called to say they benefited from the book. The experience helped me write another two books within the next 20 months. Had I listened to the disapproving comments, I would have failed in creating my own Rainbow. I would not have achieved anything except giving the satisfaction to the negative people that I achieved nothing. My colleagues' leadership guided me to develop FUN tools and books relevant to Asia.

Life is an adventure. Let us take risks not to escape life but to ensure life does not escape from us. We are only restricted by our imagination. There are no ceilings. The only ceilings that are present are the ones we put there ourselves. Life is like gardening. Gardening, they say, requires a lot of water, most of it in the form of perspiration. Leaders who lead with the spirit of adventure are free and imaginative. They are Rainbow Creators who help other people create their own Rainbow.

But risks must be taken, because the greatest danger in life is to risk nothing, The person who risks nothing does nothing, has nothing and is nothing, They may avoid suffering and sorrow, but they cannot learn, feel, change, grow, love or live. Chained by their attitudes they are slaves. They have lost their freedom. Only a person who risks is FREE.

The following poem is one we could all learn from:

Risks

To laugh is to risk
appearing to be a fool,
To weep is to risk
appearing to be sentimental,
To reach out for another is to
risk involvement,
To expose feelings is to
risk exposing your true self,
To place your ideas and your dreams,
Before a crowd is to risk their loss,
To love is to risk not being loved in return,
To live is to risk dying,
To hope is to risk despair,
To try is to risk failure.

Reflections Seven

List great leaders you admire

List their qualities

Chapter Ten:

Willing Love and Encouragement

....

"Compassion and love are not mere luxuries. As the source both of inner and external peace, they are fundamental to the continued survival of our species."

- His Holiness the XIV Dalai Lama

Unconditional Love

Some people have a way of bringing out the best in people, by their caring and the interest they take in what people do:

Are you one of them?

Some people make you feel comfortable, right from the start, for their smiles and love of life come from a warm and giving heart:

Are you one of them?

Some people are so special that whenever they are around, it seems the world is filled with happiness just waiting to be found:

Are you one of them?

These special people care, love and encourage you, for what you are, with their *unconditional LOVE!"*

These special people are winners. They are dreamers who are determined to pursue their goals with love and encouragement from friends and family. They also support their friends and family with love and encouragement so that they may pursue their dreams. Creating our own Rainbow and finding happiness in it requires the support, friendship, love and encouragement of our dear ones.

The Buddhist spiritual leader Dalai Lama said "If you want others to be happy, practise compassion. If you want to be happy, practise compassion." Though I am sharing here some incidents about family life that have affected me profoundly, love and encouragement need not be just about family life. It can relate to our friends, colleagues at work and community. I have been the beneficiary of the compassion of many people.

In a way the creation of our company, SMR, was an act of love. It was not just about making money. It was much more than that. It was about sharing our passion to help people learn and perform at the workplace. The goal was to provide employment and to encourage colleagues at work to create their own Rainbows. In my personal life I have received love and encouragement when I have been really down with the sort of depression that many people experience but do not talk about. Let me relate to you an incident.

I married late. My wife and I were unable to have children for seven years. We had seen all the doctors. It got more stressful when people started asking my wife "What is the problem?" In a society that places a high premium on having children, it created more stress. Even as the social pressure mounted, we would laugh away the question until my colleague Jeremy gave us a useful term as a reply, "We are dinkies double income, no kids." The truth was, it was becoming painful psychologically. We seldom talked about the depression we went though.

The depression only accentuated when we religiously followed whatever the doctors told us for seven years. Eventually our gynaecologist, Dr. Roopi, referred us to fertility specialist Dr. Haris Hamzah.

I could see the pain within our gynecologist when she said "I can't help you anymore and I don't have any more solutions." As I walked away from the clinic, my wife and I experienced a depression that can never be explained, but we supported one another with hope. We hoped to find happiness, which we believed, was a direction rather than a place. It was with that hope that we walked into the room of Dr. Haris.

By the time, we walked into his room, we had rehearsed what we were going to say. I started "Dr. Haris, you are our last chance. We would like to see if we can have a gift or a test tube baby." He swiveled in his chair and replied with an accent that to me sounded very American though he was a Malay and said "Oh, My God! well, well, let me tell you something. Forget about having a test tube or gift baby. First, I want you guys to take a holiday. Relax and then let us see what we can do. We can then schedule the tests and a date for the test tube baby." That is the last thing you thought you would hear from your fertility specialist. You are programmed to hear some quick fix solutions.

We followed his advice and took our first vacation to Phuket, Thailand. The vacation was a pleasant experience. We regressed to our childhood. The parachute rides, the scooter rides and the long cruises were very relaxing and enjoyable. Towards the end of the tour our guide asked us to visit the Wat Cha Long temple. She giggled and said we will most certainly visit again next year. It was later that we came to know that childless couples who visit the temple are often blessed with a child. The couple and the child usually return to pray again. We laughed about it but nevertheless visited the temple and prayed for a child.

On our return to Kuala Lumpur we visited Dr. Haris. After the checks he suggested we come back again in a week's time. When we made the return visit, he smiled and said to my wife, "We are very happy that you have conceived naturally but come back in a week." A week later, he had good news for us.

Today, we have two lovely boys and now a recent addition, a baby girl. They are a miracle and the joy of our lives. Both my wife and I survived the childless ordeal by supporting, loving and encouraging one another. Our doctor was a great guy. He did not have any ready-made prescriptions or answers but what he offered us was common sense. The act of loving, supporting and encouraging one another creates happiness. Ironically, at times we forget what a joy the boys and our daughter are, especially when they scream at not getting what they want. By the way, we did return to Phuket with our two sons to visit the Wat Cha Long temple at Phuket. We also made another trip with our daughter too. Love and encouragement can help you create your Rainbow.

Zig Ziglar, the world-renowned inspirational speaker had this to say to participants attending his talk, "To all the men in this room, I want you to go home this evening and tell your spouse what a wonderful partner you have had. Give a kiss but do not expect anything else. Make it asexual. To all the women in this room, I want you to go home this evening and tell your spouse what a wonderful partner you have had. Give a kiss but do not ask for a supplementary card. Make it asexual and non-financial."

During the coffee break, P.C. Shivdas, then the editor of the Malaysian Sunday Times, said, "You know Palan, I have not done what Zig suggests for the last 25 years. If I did it now, my wife may faint and collapse at my change in behaviour. Still, I must start acknowledging her positive contribution and thank her. Better to start now rather than never."

There is a saying that Life is not permanent. We are passing through this way now and we are not sure if we will pass through this way again. If there is any good that I can do, let me do it now.

Loving Relationships

Loving relationships develop when they are nourished regularly with love and encouragement. They help people grow.

As I was writing this book, I had an unforgettable experience. It was past midnight on Christmas Day and I was reviewing my manuscripts, furiously working on my notebook computer. It was then that I realised that my three-year-old son had sneaked into my office room in the house. My son just looked up at me and said, "Dad, what are you doing? Let us go to bed." I looked into his eyes and I could see that he desperately wanted me to go to bed. He couldn't explain the reason. I did not say another word. He wouldn't understand my arguments for staying up so late. The boy just wanted more time with me and he could not understand why I had to work so hard. That night I just got up and went to bed. That's what he wanted. I wanted to make him happy. Life revolves around your loved ones.

I am just like most fathers who leave the parenting to the mothers. However, most Sundays, I try to take both my sons out with me. We do the things that they like to do. We take either the train or the bus. I buy them ice cream. It was on one of those Sundays that I asked my eldest son, "Son, did you like visiting the supermarket and having an ice-cream?" He replied, "Yes, dad, I loved the ice-cream and the visit to the supermarket. More than that I loved the time out with you, dad."

I was really taken with that, especially coming from a three-year-old boy. I learned that, love and encouragement was not just about financial investment. It was more than that. The emotional and time investment is very important for us to help our loved ones develop the qualities of a Rainbow Creator.

On another occasion, when his kindergarten had an exhibition right in the middle of the week, in the middle of the day, I was sure I would not be able to make it. After some juggling with my schedule, I forced myself (after some gentle but forceful persuasion from my colleague Jeremy) to get to the exhibition. I could see the joy in my son when he saw me. It was so important for him that I was there. It was amazing that I was the only father around. All the other children had only their mothers accompany them. I was glad that I did not allow my priorities to be messed up. The incident was an emotional touch point. For I am as guilty as anyone else in my allocation of time. Even now, sometimes I think I have not spent as much time as I should have with them. Quality of time that you spend with your loved ones is important but so is quantity of time.

Some of my friends insist that they want a strong family but in the same breath argue they cannot have dinner with the family even once a week. The reason attributed is work pressure, lack of time, too many other social commitments, etceteras. Are we sure about what we want? My late father always said that if we cannot find time for our families, we are not getting our priorities right. This is something that always worries me. I am a regular traveller due to my work commitments. This takes me away from my family quite a bit. The justification I make is that unless I work, I will not be able to provide my family with good quality of life.

Recently I had the opportunity to travel with one of my colleagues, my multimedia developer on a long flight. He saw me working throughout the flight on my PC notebook. My colleague is a very shy person who does not really talk very much. To my surprise, he started a conversation. The conversation centred on my workaholism. He couldn't understand my justification for not spending more time with the family. My justification was that I had to work hard to provide my family good quality of life. His answer hit me real hard. He said, "Boss, you know something. The problem with fathers is that they expect to provide quality time on their terms. That is what my father did to me. We were basically a single parent family. My mother raised us. Dad was working all the time and he attributed this to needing to provide a good quality of life. What we wanted was time with him, not the cars and the money. Now he wishes he could have the old times back so that he could make amends but the time is gone. He wants it in now because he realises he is out. He won a lot in work but he wishes he had won a lot more with us in life." I was dumbfounded. That was the first time I had heard such a forceful statement from him. Surely it must have come from the deep down inside of him.

Hence, I decided then that whenever I was in town I would do things together with the family. Spend quality and quantity time with them.

We need to be there for the kids. This conversation with my colleague hit me so hard that nowadays I try to go cycling, walking, shopping and doing anything that the kids like to do. I really try to go out to see how best I can make up for the time I am away. I try to be there for them. I let them take over the leadership when I am with them. I listen to them and let me tell you; it is really difficult. But it is worth it for you can see the joy in their faces when you spend time with them. One more thing, I make sure I do not have my mobile phone with me.

Zig Ziglar said, "If you want to be close with your kids, spend half the amount of money but double the amount of time you spend with them now." Stephen Covey's highlights some very practical suggestions. I tried out one of Covey's suggestions, the power of hugs. I was unsure if it work in Asian cultures but it sure did.

Some days, when I get home, I am very tired. I walk the one-kilometre from the office to the house mainly to switch my mind off work. When I get home, I always shout out "Hey, appa (dad) is back home, please give me the hugs." The response from the children is spontaneous. When I say "Hey appa is tired, I am out of energy, they plant kisses all over my cheeks to give me energy – their style. Of course, I am supposed to be energised and interact with them now. You do not get a strong family because you wish for it. You need to want it and work on it. One of my colleagues told me the following story to persuade me to spend more time with my kids.

He had worked hard all his life to provide a good quality of life for his family. After his children had grown up, he approached his daughter and said, "Can you let me know what your impressions of me were when you were a kid?" She had no hesitation in replying "You know what, Dad, I still have this picture in my mind. We were all playing in the garden and you were there in the house working all by yourself." My colleague says his daughter's answer was painful but true. He always implores his friends to recognise the importance of spending time with the children. You need to invest time and effort to allow a relationship to grow. The importance of sincerity, honesty and sharing is important to develop any friendship. Not all of us are qualified as psychologists but we can certainly be good parents. All that is required is love, friendship and encouragement.

The story of an African American in the United States of America who loved his kids and worked all his life to educate all his daughters to qualify as doctors is an interesting one. He was hard on his children because he wanted them to create their own Rainbows. The guiding principle towards success was a single-minded devotion to his goals and discipline to create their Rainbows. When he was criticised for being hard on his family, he had this to say "If loving my family is wrong, then I do not want to be right." He was proud when his children qualified as professionals.

He would visit his daughter who worked as a doctor in a hospital. He would ask the receptionist to page his daughter over the public announcement system. He would stand there and delight in hearing his daughter's name and his surname reverberating through the public announcement system. When his daughter asked him, "Dad, do you have to do that all the time? Can't you telephone me?"

He would just reply, "The dream was to hear my daughter being addressed as a doctor over the public announcement system. I have waited for this moment for 20 years."

Willing love and encouragement water the growth of a person. There is a famous Chinese saying, "A mother can make a wonderful meal without food." The miracle of the Chinese bamboo tree is amazing. You plant the seed and you see nothing for four years except a tiny shoot corning out of a bulb. During the four years, the growth is under the soil. There is a massive fibrous root structure that spreads deep and wide under the earth. Then in the fifth year, the Chinese bamboo tree grows up to 80 feet. Many things in life are like the Chinese bamboo tree. You need to invest time and effort; you need to be patient and keep working before you see any results.

There are friends who ask me if I have human failings. Of course, I am as human as anyone else is. I have made many mistakes but I try to learn from them. There are times when I have displaced my anger on my wife for no fault of hers or vented anger on a colleague at work. I have displayed the male chauvinistic ego. The only thing that I try to do is not to repeat the behaviour. Self-awareness and my prisms help me prevent such incidents from being repeated.

I have also made many blunders. I have lost a few friends. My practice of trying to please everyone is the root of the problem. I have learned in life that this is virtually impossible. You have to learn to say 'NO' and explain the reasons why you are doing so. Life would be a lot easier if we only know when to say 'yes' and when to say 'no'.

While I was writing this book, my wife wanted me to go out for lunch. I couldn't say 'no'. Later, when I got home, I was rushing to meet my manuscript submission deadline. As I finished the book and put it on the spell check, the notebook crashed and I lost about three hour's work. I turned to my wife and said "If only we had skipped the lunch, this would not have happened." It did not take me long to realise my mistake. Within a couple of minutes, I apologised. She accepted my apology as she understood my stress and was willing to forgive me for my foolishness. I could have easily said, 'no'. Instead, I agreed to go for lunch to the restaurant and then blamed my wife for something that was no fault of hers. I ended up reacting instead of being proactive, which could have been easily avoided in the first place.

I strongly believe in the Emotional Bank Account. I do make withdrawals. However, I try to ensure that my deposits are much more than the withdrawals. I try to do small things that will reinforce love, friendship and demonstrate my commitment to my loved ones and friends. The deposits encourage people. To regularly do many small things is not a small thing. Little acts of kindness go a long way towards building relationships and unconditional love. I learned from a friend to send a card or a small gift to friends so that they know they are in my thoughts. There can never be enough red roses in a relationship. When we decide to become friends there is bound to be different expectations. Friendship is about giving and receiving, it is a two way process.

I know of a husband and wife team whom we will call Shirley and Vincent. They have a true partnership. Vincent suffered bad losses in business. Shirley was a housewife with a secondary school education. She recognised that Vincent was in financial difficulty. There was no need to explain the nature of the difficulties. She understood the unspoken problems by just listening to what Vincent could not tell her. In Asia, where the male is seen as the breadwinner, it is incredibly difficult for the male ego to ask for help from a woman. But with Vincent and Shirley it was not a battle of egos but a partnership of love.

Shirley came out of the house to help her partner create his own Rainbow. This meant getting up as early as five in the morning, caring for her three school-going children and then rushing to work. She did not complain about the 16¬ hour days as she was supporting her partner.

Today, after 10 years, the family is successful. They have recovered from their financial problems. The boys have graduated from college. My mentor, Sam Abishegam used to say "The family that prays together stays together." Shirley's family prayed and stayed together. Not for a moment was Shirley willing to think about failure. She knew as a mother that love and encouragement could provide the nourishment for success.

I have been blessed with some great friends. Friendship can support you and help you grow into a better person. There have been many friends that have gone out of their way to help me succeed in my career and life. My heart cries out and says thanks to them.

Words like "Thank you", "Please, can I help you?" "Is there something that I can do for you?" go a long way towards cementing friendships. Any relationship can survive problems with words such as "I am sorry" or "Please forgive me". These words are available to all of us. Only YOU can make use of them.

Unexpected acts of kindness create untold joy. On Mother's Day, last year, I got both my sons and nephews to choose a present for their mothers. On that day, my sons and nephews greeted their mothers in the morning with a special gift and gave them the day off.

I try my best to make my colleagues and family happy with some unexpected gifts, when they least expect it. The goal of my work life is to build a dedicated team that will help our customers learn to perform effectively. I am convinced you can only create your own Rainbow with the support of your work team.

Love and support helps turn ordinary people into extraordinary performers. At our company, SMR, we all work as a team. We have numerous problems every day but they are easily overcome by remaining positive, pragmatic and taking a supportive approach. Recently, a close friend hurt me with the following statement, "You run a circus." Though I was willing to accept feedback for growth, the way he said it was painful. The pain was even more acute as he was a beneficiary of the 'circus'. However, we do not let it bother us. Circus performers are great professionals whose job is to make other people happy. The achievements rather than the negative remarks are what matter to us most. The fact that we have made a positive contribution and are working towards what we want is more important than the negativity that is being hurled at all of us every day. Remember the lines – the ones who think it can't be done should not stand in the way of those who think it can be done.

Vision backed by values drives us to work towards being Rainbow Creators. There is the famous incident of a Spiderman scaling the world's tallest building. The Press, the city officials and the public were amazed at his skills. The moment he scaled the world's tallest building, the people who had gathered to witness the event applauded loudly. The Spiderman, when asked by the waiting journalists as to what keeps him going, replied "The positive support and applause is the encouragement that keeps me going."

Friends who provide positive support are a great source of inspiration. They guide you, provide you with unconditional love. It is important to build bridges of friendship rather than walls for sustained personal growth. You can easily communicate with your friends if you trust and love one another. Friends are people who are honest enough to give you feedback that will help you grow. Neither the friend nor you are too worried about what will happen if a friend gives honest feedback. The bridge of friendship allows you free movement while the walls we build among ourselves restrict our communication and movement. There are friends with whom we can talk about anything and everything and feel comfortable about it. On the contrary, we may know people who we may call as friends only to discover that it is impossible to trust and communicate with them.

Jesuit priest Father John Powell from Loyola College, Chicago says that if you can tell your friend "I like me best when I am with you", then your friend is an essential ingredient to creating your rainbow.

Silent games and arguments do not contribute to the growth of relationships. On the contrary, they bum the bridge of friendships. Stephen Covey says, "Love is a verb." It is about listening, sacrifice and empathy. Love is an intention. The choice to love is ours. We choose to love.

I remember friends that I had lost because we had built walls instead of bridges due to small differences. I did not know how to manage my emotions and how to act on my intentions. Rather than resolve small differences, we engaged in silent games, arguments and eventually we lost the friendships. You only realize your stupidity on hind sight. Relationships become difficult when people do not recognise that we are bound to have different expectations. The relationship gets stronger when we become aware of the differences. An inability to understand or communicate expectations leads to conflicts. A willingness to sit down and listen to one another will result in many problems being solved. Life is too short for us to waste our time fighting over our differences.

At times we know what to do but we procrastinate because of ambivalence. Ambivalence stalks us throughout life. The inability to decide what we want is a major problem. We need to get rid of the ambivalent feeling and be firm in what we want. Once, I had a discussion with one of my colleagues, who is an outstanding performer. The long discussion centred on some personal difficulties, which promoted a lot of ambivalence resulting in indecision. After the discussion, my colleague got up and said, "Let me go and first find myself." Though friends can provide you with tremendous support in your journey to create your own Rainbow, you need to know what you want and go after it with a single-minded devotion.

Friendship is the ability to withstand one another's anger so long as the anger is not a regular accurence. It is about giving and receiving. Remember the Emotional Bank Account. A learned Islamic scholar quotes from the Hadith, "In difficult times, the winner is not the one who smashes his or her opponent but the one who controls his or her anger." Anger is a hurricane that blows out the lamp of the mind. The fundamental message of love cannot be ignored for building relationships.

I was at Los Angeles airport when I saw an old man who was trying to rush back home to be with his family for Thanksgiving. As his turn on the line came, he gave his credit card to pay for the ticket. To his horror, the credit card was not honoured. I could see his disappointment. To help him, I paid the US$230 for his ticket. He gave me his address and promised to mail me a cheque within a week.

I could see the delight in his eyes. He assured me that his family would be picking him at the other end. That was it. I forgot completely about the whole incident. Honestly, I was not sure of getting the money back. A week later, his cheque was in my mail with a big thank you card. I felt very happy that I was able to help him. You can certainly make a difference through love and encouragement even to strangers. There have been instances when people have let me down but life is all about trust. I remember when a famous speaker borrowed money citing urgency with a promise to repay but never did. I knew his personal and public image was at odds. But, you cannot live a life on the basis of a negative experience. You need to consider life from a positive angle.

Ajay, my friend who lives in Chicago, told me an unfortunate story of a petrol station owner. On a very cold night, Ajay had stopped at a petrol station to fill his car with petrol. Both his young sons were with him. As he stepped out of the car, he accidentally locked the car. The kids were in the car and the engine was off. It was freezing outside. In desperation, he rushed to the petrol station owner to use his telephone. All that he wanted to do was to make a free emergency call to the police. The petrol station owner refused to allow the use of the telephone. Luckily, a police patrol car saved the situation for Ajay.

Credibility is when
Personal Self and
Public Self are congruent

They managed to unlock the doors and the children were saved. There are still some people out there, like the petrol station owner. There are not the best role models.

Martin Luther King, the civil rights hero who followed Gandhi's path of non-violence, brought hope to the African Americans in his country. Non-violence does not attempt to humiliate the opponents but to win over their friendship and understanding. The attack is directed against the forces of evil rather than the people who commit the evil. Love and encouragement aims to influence people positively. They develop the self-¬image of the people and help them change their outlook towards life with the aim of creating their rainbow.

When I wrote my first book, *The Magic of Making Training FUN!!*, many people were intrigued about the use of FUN in learning. FUN is a powerful stimulus. It is a great tension reliever. The bio-chemicals produced as a result of laughter alters moods. It gives us a sense of pleasure and relief from pain. A good friend of mine always laughs the loudest when the problems are the toughest. Humour humanises relationships. It provides relationships with fun and stability.

Rainbow Creators build friendships; they give and receive love and encouragement, as they desire to help others create their own rainbows while they are developing their own. Remember the saying; if you want to care for a few butterflies, you better start caring for a few caterpillars.

part three

Chapter Eleven:

Creating Your Own Rainbow – the Future

....

"God grant me the serenity

To accept the things I cannot change,

The courage to change the things I can,

And the wisdom to know the difference. "

Start Anew

The ultimate pursuit of every person is to create the rainbow - seek the happiness that we want, do the things that we desire and make the world a better place to live in by loving and supporting friends and family. The lessons that we learned in the last two parts and ten chapters are that none can improve your lot, if YOU do not. And let us remember that small deeds done are much better than great deeds planned. So let us start anew today.

Learning to Walk

When my wife Kamu and I had our first son, Maha, after seven years of our marriage, it was a dream come true. Within another year our second son, Subbu, arrived. Now, we have another daughter Shrieeya Sethu. We then did not know the struggles of raising children though it was certainly fun looking after them.

One day, there was great joy at home. Everyone was happy and excited. Our son Maha had embarked on an important mission in life of attempting to walk. He had not yet walked by himself but he had just attempted it and everyone was overjoyed. It is amazing to see a baby walk for the first time. If you have seen one, you will remember how determined the baby was, the self-belief and the willingness to try and to learn a new skill. Though the baby does not know it at that point, walking is a much-needed skill in life, the baby may fall a few times but it does not give up trying.

You also probably remember seeing the support, love and encouragement the baby received from family and friends. All of us applauded, cheered and encouraged Maha to walk just a little more. The applause and laughter is most welcome as it develops the baby's self-belief and self esteem. All of us wish that we could have this kind of support throughout our life. There was also another important part of this joyful event. Maha fell over. None of us ever blamed him, scolded him or called him names. Everyone rushed to help and encourage him to try again. And, before anyone could notice, the young champion was up and trying to achieve what he wanted - to learn to walk.

Creating Your Own Rainbow is about learning to 'walk again'. It is about letting go the difficulties in the past and trying to develop into the 'best' person you can be. You do not want to be 'on your knees' all your life like an infant; you want to walk confidently like an adult. Whether you will do it depends on YOU.

We all desire to do many things but we lack the perseverance. Mostly we do what we like to do or are comfortable with rather than what we ought to do. Doing the things that we need to do may be very stressful but it is important for us to walk towards success. For isn't success about the person who toiled when everyone else rested? The Chairman of my Doctoral Committee, Professor Dr. Sam Alstyne, used to remark "You can't be brave if you only have the wonderful things and forget about the painful matters in life."

YOU have read the ideas presented in this book. If you have assimilated them, you can put them into practice. No one else can. I always point out to people the concept of 'Swiss cheese' which means you take little bites, one bite at a time. Try to do things a little bit better and a little bit differently than what you did yesterday and you will see the results. Remember Lao Tze's saying "The journey of a thousand miles begins with a small step."

Uncertainty

Some people say the future is unpredictable but Alan Keys, a famous author says the best way to predict the future is to invent it. Why not go out and do it? The founder of Hotmail, netwizard Sabeer Bhatia developed *Hotmail* when he was only 27 years old and sold Hotmail to Microsoft for a cool US$400 million. Friends called him a superior human being. However, Sabeer says, "I am not superhuman, I am just persistent, determined, focussed and disciplined. I listened to legends such as Steve Jobs of Apple, Scott McNealy and Vinod Khosla of Sun Microsystems. I realised that they were human too. If they can do it, I can do it." Only a few years back, he was unsure of the future. He was in a new country in the United States of America having arrived from India with only US$250, the amount allowed by the Indian Government at that time for students pursuing an overseas education. None of the uncertainties prevented him from creating the future with Hotmail. According to him, he pondered what the Net could do for him and what he could do for the Net. Then he had an idea and the concept of Hotmail was born. Few people would buy his idea. Nineteen doors had slammed in his face. There were not many venture capitalists then who believed the Net would take off at this pace. Sabeer Bhatia would not let uncertainties or the lack of resources prevent him from creating his own Rainbow.

College dropout Steve Jobs created a computer revolution with his mouse and the Apple computer. Now with the IPod, Steve Jobs has done it again. Another Harvard dropout, Bill Gates, created the PC revolution with his DOS operating system. And, now it is the Linux operating system and the Internet. Time and tide waits for no one. Innovation and change does not stop. The question is what are you going to do about it?' Throughout the book we talked about the seven stages of Life Management essential to developing into Rainbow Creators.

The Seven Stages of Life Management:

Rainbow Components	**Vision**
1. **R**ecognising you make a difference	You hold the key to your success.
2. **A**uthentic Change	You need to embrace change for success.
3. **I**nvoking your Determination	Your persistence will drive you towards sucess.
4. **N**ever give up on yourself	Your opinion of yourself will decide.
5. **B**elief in Desire and Enthusiasm	Your passion to achieve your goals is the key to success.
6. **O**ptimal Leadership & Adventure	Your ability to lead others with zeal takes you towards your Rainbow.
7. **W**illing Love & Encouragement	Your ability to inspire and motivate people is an essential ingredient to building your Rainbow.

These seven stages of Life Management will help you create your own Rainbow and succeed in life.

THE WINNING SPIRIT

Success is not only about driving the Mercedes, material wealth or a sprawling house, it is much more than that. It is about achieving what you set out to and also about making a positive contribution to society. It is about identifying what you want, putting the effort to achieve it and making sure it is in line with your value systems. Success is much more than materialistic winning. Winning is described as an event. Being a winner is a spirit. Remember the saying "There are some defeats more triumphant than victories." Some people are winners and they have a strong value system and values can communicate goodness.

Let me tell you about an incident from the Olympics. In the yacht racing event, Lawrence Lemieux stopped racing to help a fellow competitor get out of trouble. His concern for the safety of a fellow competitor was more important than winning the gold medal. There were people who said he had wasted all the years of training because he stopped to help a fellow human being. Though he did not win the gold medal, he still came out a winner. He was remembered for keeping the Olympic spirit alive. This is what prompted Dr. Daniel Goleman to stress to us the importance of *EQ (Emotional Intelligence) over IQ (Intelligence Quotient).*

EMOTIONAL INTELLIGENCE

I remember the 1990 American Society of Training & Development International Conference in Orlando, Florida. The conference buses picked up the delegates daily at the various hotels and transported them to the conference venue. Though the waiting was long for the buses and the weather was very hot, one of the African American drivers was always in great humour. He would always greet every passenger, "Hi! Good Morning! How is it going?" When we stepped off the bus, he would always say, "Have a nice conference!" One of our customers, Mr. G Duraiswamy, a Plant Manager with Sabah Forest Industries, found it very amusing and artificial. Not for long though. At the end of the week, Mr Duraiswamy was beginning to respond to the driver's greetings. The highlight of the week was when Mr. Duraiswamy responded, "Thank you, we are leaving today and we are going to miss your smile." Daniel Goleman considers people like this driver truly successful at what they do. They are true Rainbow Creators.

Contrast this with people with very high IQ's and outstanding grades who fail miserably in what they do. Daniel Goleman narrates the story of a secondary school student with very high grades who stabbed his teacher for giving him lower than usual grade. Psychologists today say that high IQ only contributes towards 20 percent of a person's success. The remaining 80 percent comes from other factors such as EQ or emotional intelligence.

There are five factors that make up Emotional Intelligence. I think they are very relevant to creating our own Rainbows.

1. Self-awareness
2. Mood management
3. Self-motivation
4. Impulse control
5. People skills

Self-Awareness

When I trained to be a counsellor, one of the key learning points was to be aware of your own feelings and the feelings of those who need counselling. People who are aware of their own emotions are better able to navigate their lives. There are many people who are angry about an annoying incident for hours after the incident. Self¬-awareness helps us evaluate our feelings and change them. Early in my career, I found out that I tended to withdraw into my shell whenever I was stressed. A few years of evaluating myself together with feedback from my prisms helped me get out of the trap.

Mood Management

Mood changes are a fact of life. Like happiness, anger also is a normal human response but one that disrupts relationships. There is enough evidence today that outbursts of rage leave you more angry, not less. On the contrary, 'reframing' is a technique that enables you to see the situation positively rather than negatively. Praying and reflecting on your action helps you manage your moods better. Life is all about balance of moods.

Recently I had a colleague who had done a poor job. Months of work and precious money went down the drain. It was all simply because her concentration was not on the job but elsewhere. However, in the past, she had been a remarkable worker who had consistently turned in good performances. The problem now was her inability to concentrate on her work. My problem was the inability to give constructive feedback and manage my moods. I was furious, lapsed into silence and withdrew into my shell. My self-awareness helped me realise that was not the way to deal with the situation. I learned to deal with the problem professionally by reflecting upon what had happened by giving her specific feedback.

Self-Motivation

The feeling of enthusiasm, confidence and happiness is essential for achievement. Rainbow Creators are self¬ motivated. They have clear goals, an optimistic and a can-do attitude. Most athletes say they are ordinary people who turn in extraordinary performances only because they believe that they can do it. There are times when we tend to see the negative rather than the positive. Reframing techniques can help us develop into positive thinkers.

Impulse Control

The ability to self regulate your impulses is an important trait for success. You can build your resistance towards impulses through practice. This is one of the most important factors to keep yourself 'rational' and 'emotionally positive'. A trainer friend of mine was very upset recently that the customer did not provide him lunch. He displaced his anger on one of the junior supervisors. There was no doubt that the inability to control his impulse will harm his career. Sure enough, the customer never invited him again to conduct a seminar for them.

People Skills

Rainbow Creators are skilled in dealing with people. We communicate happiness and joy by the way we deal with people. We also communicate rudeness and negative attitudes by the way we interact with people. Many a time at airports, I find people very impatient with ticketing clerks. I have always found that when you deal with them patiently and politely, they respond to you better. Remember that life is an echo. People treat you nicely if you treat them nicely. The ability to get along with people will be one single quality that will separate winners from losers. If you consistently have problems with people, rather than blame others, it is time for you to evaluate your own people skills.

Create Your Own Rainbow

Live up to the human spirit. Let your imagination take over. Life is not about how many times you failed but how many times you were able to bounce back with renewed energy. Dare to dream. When a person is determined to create his/her own rainbow, no one can stop him/her.

- Put him in a prison cell - and you have Nelson Mandela.
- Bury him in the snow - and you have George Washington.
- Take away her sight and ability to hear - and you have Helen Keller.
- Threaten him with violence - and you have Mahatma Gandhi.
- Attempt to conquer him - and you have President Nasser
- Load him with racial prejudice - and you have Martin Luther King.
- Put her in a poor slum - and you have Mother Theresa.
- Murder her husband - and you have President Corazon Aquino.
- Make him a second fiddle in an obscure orchestra - and you have Toscanini.

Love yourself and treat yourself well. Know what you want and intensify your desire to achieve your goals. Remain enthusiastic. Enjoy what you do. Build bridges of friendship. Never doubt for a moment, that you can build your own Rainbow.

Hardships and struggles do not by itself make a person great. It is people's adherence to enthusiasm and faith that makes them great. Michelangelo, the great Italian painting master and sculptor spent countless hours lying on his back and taking great pains to paint the details of each figure on the lofty ceiling of the Sistine Chapel. The chapel frescoes are considered as one of the masterpieces in the world. His friend questioned him about the need for such detail, as the paintings will only be seen from a distance. "After all," the friend said, "who will know whether all the details are precise or not? Who will care if the work is perfect or not?"

"I will" replied Michelangelo, very calmly.

- The only person who will know if you have made a difference
- The only person who will know if you have done your best
- The only person who will know your internal drives
- The only person who will know or remember everything you have done
- The only person who can be honest with yourself
- The only person who can fully appreciate your efforts and attention to detail
- The only person who can honestly evaluate your performance
- The only person who can decide if you want to create your own rainbow IS YOU!

Remember *Creating Your Own Rainbow* is all about you. You have the power within you to lead the life you want. Forget about yesterday, it has lapsed. To shape the future, start today. Focus on the Now! To make a new beginning, recognise life truly is eternal today. Make the best use of it.

You alone will determine your destiny in this world. It is all about you. Destiny is not a matter of chance; it is a matter of choice. It is not a thing to be waited for; it is a thing to be achieved. You have your destiny in YOUR HANDS.

The following poem captures the spirit of translating our thoughts into action, as time will not wait for us.

When as a child I laughed and wept
Time crept!
When as a teenager I dreamed and talked
Time walked!
When I became an adult
Time ran!
Then as with the years I grew older
Time flew!
Soon I shall find as I travel on
Time gone!
And so, it is now time
To Create My Own Rainbow.

Thanks to each one of you

for joining me in this

journey to

create Rainbows

Good Luck

Kalam

Book References

- Sharma, Robin, *"The Monk Who Sold His Ferrari : A Fable* About Fulfilling Your Dreams and Reaching Your Destiny" (New York : HarperCollins Publishers Inc. – 1999)

- Tolle, Eckhart, *"The Power of Now: A Guide to Spiritual Enlightenment"* (CA : New World Library; Unabridged Edition – 2001)

- Khera, Shiv, *"You Can Win: Winners Don't Do Different Things They Do Things Differently"* (UK: Pearson Education Limited – 1998)

- Kataria, Madan, *"Laugh For No Reason"* (Mumbai: Madhuri International – 2002)

- Goleman , Daniel *"Emotional Intelligence : Why It Can Matter More Than IQ"* (Bantam - 1997)

- Hanna, Paul *"Don't Give Up!"* (Penguin Global – 2005) Kouzes, James M & Posner, Barry Z. "The Leadership Challenge" (CA : Jossey-Bass, 2003)

- Hill, Napolean *"Think & Grow Rich"* (NY : Ballantine Books – 1996)

- Maltz, Maxwell *"Psycho-Cybernetics, A New Way to Get More Living Out of Life"* (Pocket – 1989)

- Ziglar, Zig *"See You At The Top"* (LA : Pelican Publishing Company – 1982)

- Rubinstein, Moshe F & Firstenberg Iris R *"The Minding Organisation: Bring the Future to the Present and Turn Creative Ideas into Business Solutions"* (NY: John Wiley & Sons – 1999)

- Hill, Napoleon & stone, Clement W. *"Success Through A Positive Mental Attitude"* (NY: Prentice Hall – 1960)

Creating Your Own Rainbow

Creating Your Own Rainbow

I stumbled along the corridors of life
When I realised,
I didn't have an owner's manual to run my life
But I had myself.

I received a body, I had no choice
But I was aware it was the only thing
I was sure to keep for the rest of my life
And I learned to like myself.

My father told me "Son, don't compare yourself with others,
For you can make a difference and be a special person."
But he didn't stay with me, throughout my life
Yet I had myself.

You have a dream, keep hoping, and keeping trying
The sky is the limit, I was told, so did I
Trying to change the world for others and me
And I forgot myself.

I got up every morning and rushed through life.
I talked about high tech, I had no time for neighbours or prayers
I was too busy all my life
And I lost myself.

When problems tumbled on me and my self-image was dented
In despair, I blurted "Oh! God, why can't you help me?"
And God answered:"But son, you didn't ask me."
Now I remember my best help comes from myself.

I learned to admit I am less than perfect
And, show my determination desire and enthusiasm,
To try to be the BEST I can be
For it all starts with myself.

I learned not to shut out love
For it is possible to find love
The quickest way to lose it is to hold it tight
The surest way to keep it is open up yourself

Look for the roses in your loved ones
Show them the beauty of life
Friends make up your life
Take them on this Rainbow journey with yourself.

Life provides the canvas, you do the painting
Take charge of your life or someone else will,
Don't run through life so fast,
That you forget yourself.

Life is not a race but a Rainbow
To be created and witnessed at every stage of life
In this possibility journey
What matters most is your SELF.

About the Author:

R. Palan Ph. D.

The son of a Malaysian father and Indian mother, Palan grew up in a multicultural environment; he studied chemistry, professional medical and psychiatric social work, psychology and management. He lived and worked in five countries.

He wandered through the corridors of life when his father died abruptly. His friends and family supported him in pursuing his goals in life - studying, working and building his career. A trained professional speaker and human capital development consultant, Palan has written several books, produced videos, created management games, pioneered the use of FUN in training and produced the internationally acclaimed software HRDPower.

A frequent traveller, Palan has spoken to thousands of people in thirty over countries over the last three decades. Palan is the Chairman and CEO of SMR Technologies Berhad, a company listed on the MESDAQ Market of the Kuala Lumpur Stock Exchange. The company has offices and representatives in USA, Singapore, United Arab Emirates, Brunei and India.

Palan lives in Kuala Lumpur, Malaysia with his wife Kamu, two sons Maha and Subu and daughter Shrieeya. He also travels extensively to Dubai, U.A.E. and Chicago, USA.

More details on his website www.palan.org

www.ingramcontent.com/pod-product-compliance
Lightning Source LLC
LaVergne TN
LVHW050642100826
845148LV00011B/1955

* 9 7 8 1 5 9 9 3 2 0 6 4 9 *